D0601624

Style at *Home*

The Best of Today's Creative Home Arts

CREATIVE
HOME
ARTS
—CLUB—

Creative Home Arts Library™

Style at Home
The Best of Today's Creative Home Arts

Printed in 2007.

Creative Director
Tom Carpenter

Managing Editor
Heather Koshiol

Book Design
Jenya Prosmitsky

Book Production
Teresa Marrone

3 4 5 6 / 09 08 07
ISBN 10: 1-58159-280-9
ISBN 13: 978-1-58159-280-1
© 2006 Creative Home Arts Club

CREATIVE
HOME
ARTS
—CLUB—

Creative Home Arts Club
12301 Whitewater Drive
Minnetonka, Minnesota 55343
www.creativehomeartsclub.com

Contributing Writers
Kristen Berget
Karen Blonigen
Simone Chisholm
Margaret Hanson-Maddox
Nancy Hoerner
Mary Beth Kissling
Marcene Kruger
Lion Brand Yarn
Jan Page
Kathryn Wiley
Linda Wyszynski

Contributing Photographers
Scott Jacobson
Lion Brand Yarn
Greg Page/Page Studios

Special Thanks To:
Mike Billstein/Color Co., Terry Casey, Janice Cauley, Karen Jackson, Bill Nelson (Stitch Illustrations), Kelly O'Hara, Happi Olson.

Contents

Introduction

Issue after issue, Members tell us what they love most about *Today's Creative Home Arts* magazine—the variety of projects, the beautiful photography and the clear step-by-step instructions that help turn all your crafting and home decorating efforts into big successes.

This book proudly brings together a collection of "best of the best" projects from *Today's Creative Home Arts*. **Style at Home** makes it easy for you to find great craft and decorating projects that will bring personal style and creativity into your home. Here are 40 wonderful projects, ready and waiting for your attention, energy and creativity!

Start with **Paint with Pizzazz,** and use decorative painting designs and techniques to create projects from scratch or refresh items already in your home. **Nifty Stitches** presents you with a wonderful collection of attractive knitting, needlepoint and embroidery projects. **Sewing with Style** helps you get your sewing machine humming with creations that are charming and personal. **Creative Crafts** offers a multitude of fun projects you can make for yourself or someone special. In **Designer Decorating,** discover great ways to add style everywhere in your home … plus outside in your garden! Finally, **Makeover Magic** shows you how to achieve the results you want with the budget you have.

Style at Home will live up to—and surpass—your expectations for a Creative Home Arts Club publication. Full-size color photos of the finished projects show you what you're working toward. Step-by-step pictures and clear illustrations guide you through the creative process without a hitch. And easy-to-follow written instructions lead you through each project, while answering all your creative questions.

Where you go from here is up to you! To start, just page through and let yourself be inspired. It's time to add some personal style throughout your home … and into your everyday living. Get creative—and get creating—with *Style at Home.*

CREATIVE
HOME
ARTS
—CLUB—

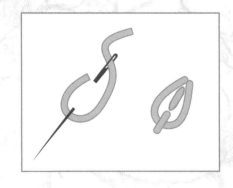

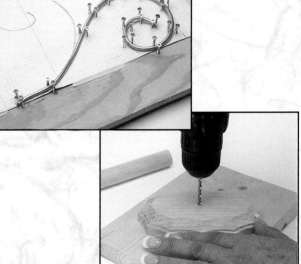

Paint with *Pizzazz*

Paint adds dimension and communicates a mood—from a soft and elegant whisper to a bright and lively shout. Paint can also transform old, tired items into fresh new pieces. The projects in this chapter help you infuse custom style with paint. See how to personalize a shower curtain, renew an old trunk or create charming painted decor for your home or garden. Express your style with color!

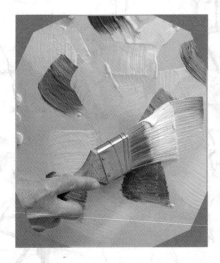

Painted *Paradise*

Can't find a shower curtain you like at a store? Fabric paint pens let you create what you want, when you want.

In a bathroom, the shower curtain is a dominant piece of decor. So what do you do when you can't find the perfect premade shower curtain to match your style? Simple. A plain cotton curtain, stencils, and fabric paint pens will let you create almost any image you wish, in the colors you want.

Although we did this project on a shower curtain, you can use the same techniques on other home decor items such as curtains, or simply create a similar design on clothing.

You Will Need

- 100-percent cotton shower curtain (this type is used with a second liner inside)
- One or more stencils in a style of your choice
- Permanent fabric paint pens in both wide and fine-tip (we used DecoFabric pens by Marvy-Uchida)
- Painter's tape

1 It's easiest to plan your design if you have a large table where you can spread your shower curtain out from side to side.

Our curtain had a faint grid pattern on it as part of the weave, so that helped us visualize our final design. If your curtain doesn't have such a grid, you'll need to measure from the bottom and sides of the curtain to create a symmetrical design.

Once we had our design in mind, we marked the positions and colors we intended to paint on pieces of painter's tape, and then placed those so that the bottom of the stencil would rest directly on our mark.

2 It's important to create a few practice stencils on a scrap of cloth to get the feel for how your paint pens will respond. Since our shower curtain was made of a fairly roughly woven material, we practiced on the back of a piece of old jeans fabric, which had a similar feel. We tested each of our colors, and then combined them in different ways to find a design we liked. (It's also a good idea to refer to this piece while you work so that you remember which sections of the stencil receive which colors.)

3 With our paint pens, we found that the easiest way to work with our stencils was to hold the stencil firmly in place over the stretched curtain, and to apply the paint with a dabbing motion. This kept the paint flowing smoothly, and also helped keep the tip of the pen from abrading. (If this happens, simply cut off the worn portion of the felt with a sharp scissors and continue.)

Once we had colored the inside of our stencil, we removed the stencil and then outlined our butterflies and dragonflies using a fine-line paint pen in a dark color to give the stencil definition.

Once the stenciled portion of your shower curtain has dried, the images can be heat-set by ironing them. They will then remain colorfast and waterproof.

A Victorian *Trunk*

Transform a tired old trunk into an elegant accent piece.
Paint and wallpaper make it possible!

We always called this Grandpa's trunk, although in truth, it was actually his World War II foot locker. It looked as if it had been through a war, too.

If you have a battered old trunk, even one as distressed as this, don't be so quick to banish it to the garage or toss it in the garbage. With a little work and imagination, it can be transformed into a beautiful center of interest or an accent piece. Best of all, you don't have to be an artist to finish this project. We used wallpaper border images and a couple of painting techniques to create our very own Victorian treasure chest, and you can, too!

You Will Need

- Trunk*
- Painter's tape
- Primer
- Three 2-inch latex brushes
- Acrylic latex enamel for trunk base, and additional paint in light and dark accent shades
- Gold paint (we used American Accents Antique Gold paint finish kit)
- Wallpaper border or wallcovering with a large design (we used a wallpaper border by Ralph Lauren that featured moss roses)
- Utility knife and blades
- Decoupage medium (we used Mod Podge matte)
- Variety of artist paints to match
- ½ yard of scrap lace fabric
- Gold spray paint

See Getting Started, below

Optional:
- Wallpaper for lining inside of trunk
- Satin cording
- Hot-glue gun and glue

Getting Started

Our trunk was thin metal around a wooden frame, and it had significant rust on it. We used several products to repair the trunk before we decorated it. If this does not apply to your trunk, simply proceed with the decorative aspects of this project.

SPECIAL PROJECT TIP

We found that a barbecue grill cleaning brush had nice soft bristles for removing rust, and the grate cleaner side worked great for scraping off old paint in corners.

1 OPTIONAL: Old trunks often smell musty. If your trunk has an odor, spray the inside with a product called AtmosKlear (available at your local hardware store), following manufacturer's directions, or place several bags of activated charcoal in the trunk for three days to absorb odor.

2 OPTIONAL: Remove all rust and flaking paint with a fine-toothed wire brush. We used a product by Rust-Oleum called Rust Reformer on the metal parts of our trunk to stop further rusting, following manufacturer's directions.

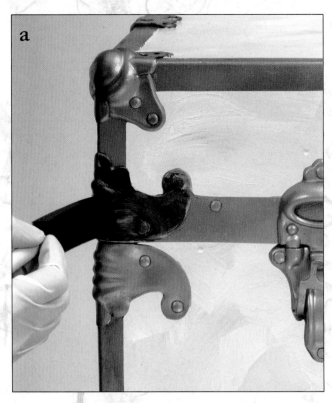

a

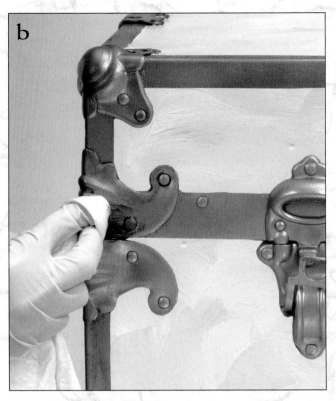

b

3 We primed our trunk with a good quality primer. We let that dry, and then painted the body using a special technique called French brush color washing. (See directions on page 13.)

Once our background was painted, we decided to emphasize some of the trunk's decorative details. Our

trunk had unique trim lining the edges, so we used an Antique Gold paint finish kit from American Accents to emphasize it. The hardware was first sprayed gold and then was brushed with a gray antiquing element (photo 3a), which we then wiped off almost completely, leaving paint only in some recessed areas (photo 3b).

SPECIAL PROJECT TIP

Cut out all your pieces of wallpaper and tape them in place on your trunk before pasting any of them. This lets you examine and change your design as you experiment with different looks.

4 Select an image from your wallpaper. Complement one or two large images such as flowers with smaller images such as leaves or buds. Place the wallpaper on a cutting surface, and use a craft knife to carefully cut out the design elements you have selected.

This technique uses three shades of latex paint—a neutral base color, a bright highlight color, and a dark shadow color. We used a light tan as our base, an off-white as our highlight, and a chocolate brown shade as our shadow.

TIP: It's a good idea to experiment with this technique and the shades you choose on a piece of tagboard before working on your trunk.

1 After priming your trunk, paint the entire piece in your base color. Let dry, and apply a second base coat to the trunk, this time using short, random brushstrokes.

2 With the same brush while your base coat is still wet, apply the highlight color with a few random strokes over the first color.

3 Select a new brush. While the paint is still wet from Steps 1 and 2, apply several random strokes of the darker color over the first coats. At this point, stand back, make sure you have good coverage with all three colors, and move directly to Step 4.

4 Take a clean brush and begin to smooth and blend the three colors, using loose figure-8 strokes, lightly touching the surface and blending the colors until the desired effect is reached. NOTE: The more you blend, the more the overall color tone will lighten. TIP: Don't blend too much.

a

b

5 After determining the best position for your design (see Tip on page 12), begin to decoupage your largest elements to the trunk (photo 5a). Apply decoupage medium to the back of the wallpaper motifs and immediately position on the trunk. Gently press and smooth out any air bubbles with your fingers and make sure all edges are sealed (photo 5b).

6 With a soft brush or sponge brush, apply a second thin coat of decoupage medium over the surface and edges of all the designs. Allow to dry thoroughly.

7 OPTIONAL: You can add your own details over the top of your decoupaged design using an artist's brush and acrylic paints. Consider adding vines, small flowers and leaves, or any detail that you liked but that was too small to cut out of the wallpaper.

8 For a soft, romantic touch to finish your trunk, lay a piece of scrap lace fabric over your finished design. Make sure the fabric lies smoothly and then tape it down to hold its position. Using a can of gold spray paint, spray VERY lightly over the surface at a distance of about 18 inches. TIP: This technique looks best if it's very subtle. Test your technique on poster board before you start on your trunk. Too much could spoil a good thing.

SPECIAL PROJECT TIP

A nice way to finish the inside of this trunk is to paper the inside using a complementary wallpaper. Use wallpaper paste to attach the paper for good adhesion. Use hot-glue to attach satin cording to the corners to hide any rough edges.

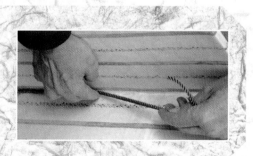

Season's Greetings

This decorative plaque welcomes guests warmly even when it's cold outside.

This easy-to-paint door decoration adds a bit of whimsy to your welcome and is perfect for displaying during the holidays and all throughout the winter months.

You Will Need

- 12-by-20-inch unfinished wood tavern sign*
- 220-grit sandpaper (fine)
- Paper towels
- 1-inch foam brush
- Wood sealer
- Sea sponge
- Tracing paper
- White and black graphite paper
- Stylus
- Pencil
- Palette or foam plate
- Brush basin
- Acrylic outdoor paint**
- Paintbrushes***
- Old toothbrush
- Outdoor dimensional snow****
- Palette knife

*We bought a wooden tavern sign by Walnut Hollow at our local craft store.
**We used weather-resistant DecoArt Patio Paint in Citrus Green, Cloud White, Concrete Grey, Daisy Cream, Golden Honey, Honest Copper, Patio Brick, Pine Green, Tango Blue, Tiger Lily Orange, Woodland Brown, and Wrought Iron Black.
***We used Loew-Cornell Golden Taklon brushes Nos. 4 and 6 flat shaders and Fabric brushes, Nos. 4 and 8 round scrubber, No. 10/0 liner.
****We used DecoArt Outdoor Snow.

Getting Started

Lightly sand entire wood plaque with sandpaper and wipe clean with a paper towel.

Using foam brush, paint the entire plaque with wood sealer and let dry. Using foam brush, paint entire plaque with one coat Cloud White and wipe gently with paper towel while wet for a whitewashed effect. Let dry.

Using sea sponge, dip into both Daisy Cream and Cloud White. Dab paint onto upper and lower areas of sign.

1 Using No. 6 flat shader brush, apply Honest Copper paint to an old toothbrush. Spatter paint onto top and bottom edges of sign by pulling fingernail across toothbrush bristles. Let dry.

a

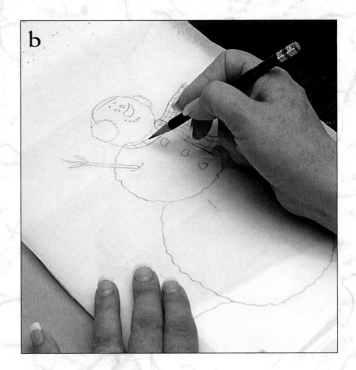

b

2 Using 1-inch foam brush, paint center section of sign Tango Blue (photo 2a). Let dry.

Trace pattern (right) onto tracing paper (photo 2b). Position traced pattern on blue portion of sign as shown at right and slip white graphite paper between surface and tracing paper. Using stylus, retrace design. Remove graphite paper.

Snowman Pattern   *Enlarge at 180%*

3 Using No. 8 round fabric scrubber, tap Cloud White snow below snowman. Let dry.

FOR THE EARMUFFS: Using No. 4 round fabric scrubber, tap in Tiger Lily Orange onto earmuff fur. Using same brush, tap in Patio Brick on left sides for shading and Cloud White on right sides for highlighting. Using liner, add headband in Concrete Grey and touch in a small line of Cloud White.

FOR THE FACE: Lay traced pattern over snowman and slip black graphite paper in between. Retrace face. Using liner brush, add Wrought Iron Black mouth and eyebrows. Using liner brush, add Tiger Lily Orange nose. Using stylus, add two Wrought Iron Black eyes.

FOR THE ARMS: Using liner brush, paint both arms Golden Honey. Using the same brush, randomly touch in some Woodland Brown for shading and some Cloud White for highlighting.

FOR THE BUTTONS: Using handle end of No. 8 round fabric scrubber brush, dip into Wrought Iron Black and touch onto body for buttons. Using liner brush, add Cloud White reflection line to each button. (See photo 4a for all.)

FOR THE BRANCH: Using No. 6 flat shader brush, dip into both Golden Honey and Woodland Brown. Paint main branch and twig. Use liner brush to make smaller limbs.

Using liner brush, dip into both Citrus Green and Pine Green to paint evergreen needles with various line lengths (see photo 4b).

Dilute Cloud White paint to milky consistency. Using No. 6 flat shader, paint this thinned paint onto toothbrush. Spatter thinned paint as "snow" over snowman and sky area.

Lay traced pattern over lettering areas and slip white graphite paper in between for "Friends" and black graphite paper in between for "Welcome." Using liner brush, paint "Welcome" in Tango Blue and "Friends" in Cloud White.

4 Using No. 4 round fabric scrubber, tap Cloud White onto body and head. Tap Concrete Grey on left side for shading. Using No. 4. round fabric scrubber, tap Concrete Grey under body on snow-covered ground.

FOR THE SCARF: Using No. 4 flat shader, paint scarf Citrus Green. Using No. 4 flat shader, shade scarf in Pine Green and highlight in Cloud White. Using liner brush, add Tiger Lily Orange plaid lines.

SPECIAL PROJECT TIP

To shade and highlight your details on this project, you'll need to "float" color onto designated areas.

To float, dip your brush into water and then lay your brush onto a paper towel until the shine leaves the bristles. Dip one side of brush into desired paint and move brush in a stationary spot in a back and forth motion on the palette to remove excess paint from brush. Place loaded side of brush along edge that is to be shaded or highlighted and apply slight pressure to the brush while pulling the brush toward you.

5 Using a palette knife, randomly apply dimensional snow to top and bottom of plaque and onto evergreen needles. Let dry completely.

To hang, attach picture hardware to back of plaque and string ribbon through to secure.

A Painted
Garden

Turn a handful of plain wooden birdhouses into a focal point in your garden.

This is one bouquet that is sure to bloom all summer in your backyard flowerbed.

Inexpensive, premade wooden birdhouses are readily available in all sorts of sizes and shapes at your local craft or hobby store. You'll find that a number of premade wooden details or accents—such as small fences, flowers, butterflies, and bugs—can also be found there very inexpensively.

We decided to combine those items to create a display that adds a bright spot of color to any yard.

The beauty of this project—besides the small cost involved for the materials—is that your finished item can be as individual as you are. We used a variety of paint techniques, including some stencils and stamps, along with leftover spray paint in several colors and the remnants of a few "almost all gone" acrylic craft paints to come up with our designs. (Get the kids involved with this project, too. Simply give each one a birdhouse to decorate, and then assemble the piece following the directions on the next page. You'll have a piece of art, and a family memento.)

You Will Need

- Variety of wooden birdhouses
- Sandpaper and soft tack cloth
- Spray paint primer and colored spray paint
- Acrylic paints
- Stamps, stencils, etc.
- Decorative wood accents such as fences or flowers
- Liquid Nails construction adhesive
- Small wooden plaques (two for each birdhouse)
- One large wooden base plaque
- 1-inch dowels
- Drill and 1-inch wood screws
- Handsaw
- Polyurethane sealer spray

1 The key to a smooth finish when painting on unfinished wood is to lightly sand the birdhouse and wipe it clean with a soft tack cloth. Prime the piece with two light coats of spray paint primer. (Place several birdhouses into a large cardboard box before spraying them to minimize mess. Be sure to fully cover all of the wood with primer.)

Once you've primed your wood, you can paint the houses with either acrylics or spray paint. Use stamps, stencils, or other decorations. We added several details to our birdhouses, such as small wood fences, by painting these pieces and then gluing them to our birdhouses using a good quality construction adhesive such as Liquid Nails.

2 To create the display for our birdhouses, we purchased several small wooden plaques at our local craft store, along with a large wooden plaque to use as our base. You need two wood plaques for each birdhouse, one to attach to the bottom of the house, and one to attach to the wood base. We also purchased several wooden dowels for our supports.

To prevent cracking the base and the dowels, predrill a hole in the center of each plaque, and then insert a 1-inch wood screw through the plaque into the dowel. **TIP:** Before you attach the bottom plaque to your dowel, spend some time evaluating how you want your finished display to appear. We found that cutting our dowels at different heights gave us the best final look. Once you've done this, attach the dowel to the second base plaque.

Prime and paint your dowels, and all of the plaques, including your wood base.

3 Turn a birdhouse upside down, and use two 1-inch wood screws to attach the wood plaque and dowel support to the bottom.

Set the birdhouse upright, and use two more 1-inch wood screws to attach the other end of the dowel and the other wood plaque to your support base.

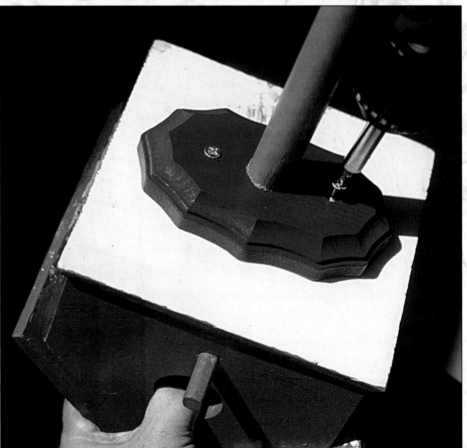

4 Depending on the size of your base, you may need to angle some of the wooden plaques to accommodate all of the bird-houses you wish to mount.

To finish and protect your display, spray several coats of polyurethane sealer over the entire piece. Coat the display thoroughly to protect the paint from the weather.

Nifty Stitches

What an elegant way to add style—cross-stitch a pretty design with colorful floss, embroider a timeless motif with rich ribbon, or knit up a soft and cozy throw. With various colors, threads, yarns and fabrics, the possibilities are endless. Exercise your creativity and add these designs to whatever sparks your imagination!

A Garden
Journal

Use this cross-stitch guide to enhance a plain sketchbook.

Summertime—and the garden's in bloom. This is a pretty way to preserve all the memories of this year's garden.

This delicate cross-stitch design is a lovely way to enhance a plain paper garden journal. We created our cross-stitch on a special fabric resembling burlap, which gives the piece added charm.

Cross-Stitch Basics

We used this design as a book cover, but you can use it on any item you wish to embellish. The design can be worked on a pillow top, the bib part of an apron, a tote bag, or box top.

Whatever use you have for this design, remember these tips:
- Be sure your design is in the center of the fabric.
- Use 16- to 18-inch length of thread.
- Separate the thread by holding the strand near the top of the cut length. With your other

hand, pull one strand straight up and away from the hand holding the thread. Remove the strands needed and join them together again.
- To begin stitching, tie a knot in the end of the thread. Go about 2 inches over on the row where the first stitch will be placed. Take the needle down through the front side of the fabric, and bring the needle up from the

back side in the lower left corner of the first stitch. When the stitching reaches the knot, clip the knot and continue to stitch. To end threads, slip the needle/thread under several stitches on the back side.
- Remove basting thread as you work the cross-stitches.
- If you prefer not to use beads, embroidery thread can be used for all cross-stitches.

You Will Need

- Journal*
- Lambswool 10-count Heatherfield cross-stitch fabric**
- Khaki poly/cotton fabric for lining
- 10 inches of violet ¼-inch ribbon
- Embroidery floss in dark blue violet, medium blue violet, dark lemon, Christmas green, parrot green, and light parrot green***
- Frosted glass beads in light yellow and purple****

- Embroidery hoop
- Terry towel
- Ruler
- Scissors
- Sewing machine
- Tapestry No. 24
- Beading needles
- Sewing thread to match
- Light color thread for basting
- Fray Check

*Ours was a 7-inch square Cachet Classic Sketch Book. To figure the fabric required for the journal you purchase, see instructions in "Preparing the Cover."

**Heatherfield Fabric, Wichelt Imports, Inc., (608)788-4600, E-mail: wichelt@wichelt.com; www.wichelt.com.

***We used DMC floss in blue violet dark No. 333; blue violet medium No. 340; lemon dark No. 444; Christmas green No. 700; parrot green medium No. 906, and parrot green light No. 907, www.dmc-usa.com.

****We used frosted and glass seed beads from Mill Hill Beads in yellow crème No. 62041 and crayon purple No. 02069, Mill Hill, (800)447-1332, www.millhill.com.

How to Work the Cross-Stitch
Follow the cross-stitch diagram, starting in the right corner of the square. At the starting point, bring the needle and thread up for 1, taking the needle across the square and down at 2. Come up at 3 and down at 4. Continue working the stitches in this manner.

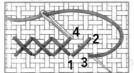

Figure 1

How to Work the Backstitch
For the stems of the flowers and leaves: Bring the needle up at 1 and go down at 2. Skip one square and bring the needle up at 3; go back across the square, going down at 4. NOTE: 1 and 4 will share the same space between squares.

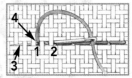

Figure 2

How to Work the Straight Stitch
For the veins of the violet and leaves: Bring the needle up at 1, go across the area and down at 2, being sure the thread lies flat. Repeat this until all the straight stitches are in place.

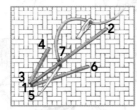

Figure 3

SPECIAL PROJECT TIP

When working the stitches, do not carry thread across open spaces since it will show. Work the border rows one row at a time so your thread will lie smooth. Clip all knots when cross-stitches are completed.

Cross-stitch pattern key

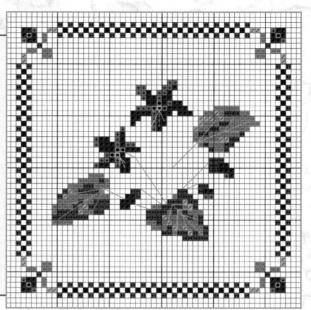

Color	Symbol	Embroidery Floss Color
	◤	blue violet dark (DMC No. 333)
	↓	blue violet medium (No. 340)
	X	lemon dark (No. 444)
	H	Christmas green (No. 700)
	≫	parrot green medium (No. 906)
	/	parrot green light (No. 907)

Backstitch Instructions:

	___	parrot green medium (No. 906) [flower and leaf stems]

Straight Stitch Instructions:

	_____	parrot green light (No. 907) [leaf veins]
	_____	lemon dark (No. 444) [flower veins]

Symbol Mill Hill Beads

	●	Frosted Glass Beads, yellow crème (No. 62041)
	·	Glass Seed Beads, crayon purple (No. 02069)

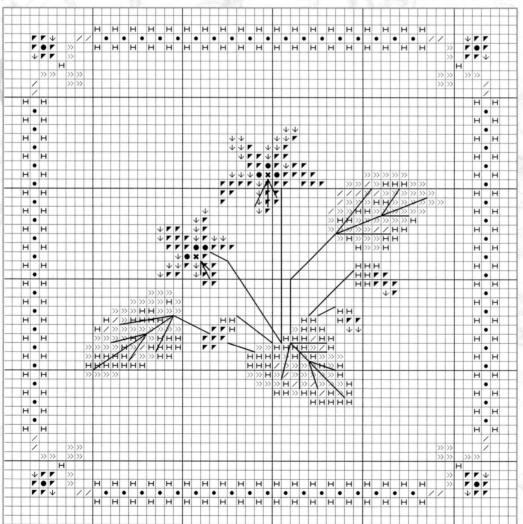

How to Center the Design

Find the horizontal center of the fabric and run a basting thread across the area. Measure 1/2 inch from the right edge of the fabric and run a vertical basting thread. Measure your journal from the spine to the edge of the cover to determine the width. From the vertical basting thread on the right,

measure over the width of the cover. You can run a basting thread at that point or mark with a pin. Find the center between these two points and run a vertical basting thread. The starting point is where the center vertical and horizontal threads cross. From the center, count up six squares to start cross-stitching the bottom of the large violet.

- Use three strands to cross-stitch and backstitch.
- Use one strand for straight stitches for veins.
- Use two strands of sewing thread to attach beads.
- Cross-stitch design is centered on right end of journal cover using colors shown on chart.

Preparing the Cover

If you want to use this design as a cover for a garden journal, cut your cover cross-stitch fabric by measuring the width of your journal from the front edge around the spine to the outer edge of the back cover. Add 1 inch to this for seam allowances ($\frac{1}{4}$ inch on each end, plus $\frac{1}{2}$ inch for ease to accommodate the thickness of the journal).

Preparing the Flaps

Measure the height of the journal from the bottom to the top edge. To this measurement, add 1 inch for the seam allowances and ease.

Cut the cover from the cross-stitch fabric and the lining fabric.

Cut two pocket flaps and lining for flaps from cross-stitch fabric and lining material. Flaps should be cut $4\frac{1}{2}$ inches wide by the height of your journal. Our flaps were $4\frac{1}{2}$ by $8\frac{1}{4}$ inches.

Use sewing thread to zigzag the edges of all of the cross-stitch fabric.

Pin one pocket flap lining and one cross-stitch flap piece with right sides together. Sew along the long edge. Turn right side out, and press along seamed edge to create a fold line. Join other pocket flap pieces in same manner.

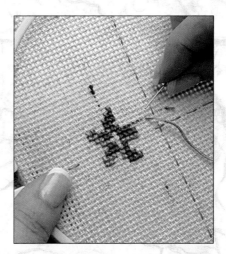

How to Attach the Beads

Follow the cross-stitch diagram to attach the bead. Come up at 1 and slide the bead in place. Take the needle down at 2, and come up at 1 again. Slide the needle and thread back through the same side of the bead as you did the first time, and take the needle down again at 2. The bead hole will be vertical when the thread is pulled into place. Pull the thread taut and continue on to the next bead, attaching it in the same manner. Be sure the fabric lies smooth after each bead is attached and that the beads are secure.

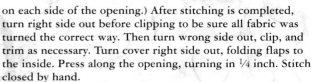

Ironing the Cover

Place a terry towel on your ironing board. Place the cross-stitch facedown on the towel and carefully press.

Assembling the Book Cover

Lay lining cover on flat surface, right side up. Place a pocket flap piece, lining side down, on each end of lining, matching raw edges. Place the cross-stitch cover right side down, matching raw edges. Pin all layers together, being sure the pin goes through all fabric. Stitch all pieces together using a $\frac{1}{4}$ inch seam allowance. Leave a $3\frac{1}{2}$-inch opening in the center bottom seam for turning. (Be sure to secure the seam line

on each side of the opening.) After stitching is completed, turn right side out before clipping to be sure all fabric was turned the correct way. Then turn wrong side out, clip, and trim as necessary. Turn cover right side out, folding flaps to the inside. Press along the opening, turning in $\frac{1}{4}$ inch. Stitch closed by hand.

Attach the ribbon to the lining on the inside of the front cover. Measure over $6\frac{1}{2}$ inches, place the ribbon, and sew to the lining about $\frac{1}{4}$ inch below the edge of the cover. Take three or four small stitches, one on top of the other. Tie off thread and trim as necessary. Place a small drop of Fray Check on the end of the ribbon.

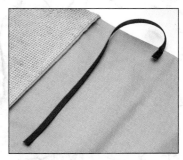

Delicate *Guest Towel*

This classic cream-on-white towel will make any guest feel like a queen.

The delicate appearance of embroidered flowers makes this hand towel elegant and impressive.

You Will Need

- Tracing paper
- Permanent pen or marker
- Mechanical pencil
- 14-by-21-inch linen/cotton towel*
- Six-stranded embroidery floss **
- Glass seed beads ***
- Embroidery needles No. 5–10 (package)
- Light box or sunny window
- Iron, straight pins, and general sewing supplies

*We used a ready-made Wimpole Street Creations Cutwork Towel (55 percent linen, 45 percent cotton) www.barrett-house.com.

**We used DMC Six-stranded Embroidery Floss in Ecru (www.dmc-usa.com).

***We used Mill Hill Glass Seed Beads No. 00123 Cream (www.millhill.com).

Getting Started

Transferring the Pattern

Press towel so that it lies flat.

Trace the pattern (Fig. 1 on page 32) onto tracing paper using a permanent pen. Then place the traced pattern on a light box or tape it to a sunny window. Center the right side of the towel over the center of the pattern, placing the center flower stem 1½ inches above the center flower of the cutwork towel. Use straight pins to secure in place. HINT: Trace only the straight line in the center of each leaf and lightly trace the center flower. Use the mechanical pencil to transfer the pattern onto the towel.

How to Work the Stem Stitch

Always keep the thread on the lower side of the needle, working the stem stitch along the drawn line. Bring the needle up at 1 and down at 2. Needle comes up at 3, halfway between 1 and 2. Continue in this manner until area is completed.

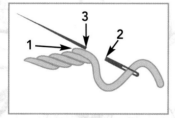

Figure 2

How to Work the Satin Stitch

Bring the needle up at 1 and go across the area, going down at 2, flush to previous stitch. Bring the needle back up at 3 next to 1. Go back across the area going down next to 2. Continue working the area in this manner.

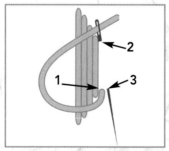

Figure 4

Lazy Daisy Variation

Bring the needle up at 1 and let your thread lie on top of the fabric, forming a loop. Holding the loop in place, go down at 2 as close as possible to 1. Bring the needle up at 3, cross over the thread, down at 4. Come back up just below 1 and 2, go across the area inside the loop and down just before 3. Repeat for each lazy daisy variation.

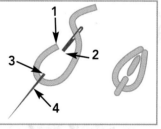

Figure 3

General Instructions:

Use two strands of ecru floss to stitch the pattern unless otherwise noted.

Use the size needle from the No. 5–10 package that you are comfortable working with to work stitches. The most important thing when using an embroidery needle is that the floss has room to move within the eye of the needle.

Begin stitching by placing two small stitches in an area that will be covered by thread as you work the embroidery stitches. End the thread by running it under several previously worked stitches.

SPECIAL PROJECT TIPS

• Tissue paper can be used instead of tracing paper to transfer your design.

• For an even more elegant look, stitch the towel in white on white, and use white beads to accent.

Embroidery Pattern
Enlarge or reduce slightly to fit your towel.

Figure 1

1 Using the stem stitch (Fig. 2) work the flower stems, leaf stems, and leaf branches. Using the lazy daisy variation (Fig. 3) work all the leaves. Keep your floss strands even and smooth as you work this stitch.

2 Using the satin stitch (Fig. 4) work the petals of the flowers with three strands of ecru floss. Start in the center of the petal working outward across the area to the outer traced edge. When one side of the petal is completed, work the other side from the center outward. Your stitches should lie flat and smooth as you work the petals.

3 Using a No. 10 embroidery needle and one strand of ecru floss, sew five No. 00123 beads in the center circle of the flowers and a single bead (Fig. 5) next to the leaf branches where indicated by a round dot. Sew through each bead twice to secure.

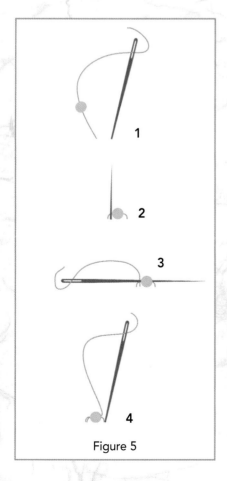

Figure 5

Picture *Perfect*

This silk ribbon frame is perfect for a special picture that is dear to your heart.

We used a plain photo mat as the framework for this silk ribbon-embellished frame to showcase a special picture.

If you're a scrapbooker, try attaching this finished mat to the front of an album for an even more impressive impact.

We purchased our easel back from a frame shop, but you can also use an easel back from an inexpensive picture frame purchased at a discount store.

You Will Need

- Eggshell crushed decorator fabric
- Tracing paper
- Permanent marker
- Mechanical pencil
- Chenille and beading needles
- 6-strand embroidery floss in violet, red, and green*
- Several shades of 4 mm Pure Silk Embroidery Ribbon **
- Glass Seed Beads ***

- Pellon Fusible Featherweight to Medium Fusible Interfacing
- Oval mat with a 5-by-7-inch opening in an 8-by-10 frame
- 8-by-10-inch picture frame easel back
- Poly-fil traditional batting
- Painter's tape and Photo Corners
- Aleene's Fast Grab Tacky Glue
- Iron, straight pins, general sewing and crafting supplies

*We used DMC floss, No. 553 Violet, No. 666 Bright Red, and No. 702 Kelly Green (www.dmc-usa.com).

**We used 4 mm Bucilla Pure Silk Ribbon, No. 113 Dark Lilac, No. 536 Deep Red (optional), No. 539 Red, No. 638 Parrot Green and No. 642 Light Emerald (www.plaidonline.com). Note: Red ribbon No. 539 can be used for all the roses and buds.

***We used Mill Hill Glass Seed Beads No. 02085 Brilliant Orchid (www.millhill.com).

Silk Ribbon Basics

When working with silk ribbon, secure the ribbon (Fig. 1) in the needle's eye. To begin stitching, leave a loose inch of ribbon hanging on the back of the work. After the first stitch, bring the needle/ribbon to the back side and pierce the loose tail with the needle. Pull the ribbon through the tail to secure.

For the spider rose (Fig. 2), take a small stitch (leaving a tail) in the area you will weave over, and secure by piercing the tail. To end ribbon, run it under a couple of stitches and pierce to secure.

Use your thumb to keep the ribbon flat as it goes into the fabric. The secret of a beautiful stitch is keeping the ribbon flat as it comes from the back of the fabric and goes down into the fabric.

Figure 1: Threading the Needle

Use a 10- to 12-inch piece of ribbon; pull the thread through the eye about 3 inches. Pierce the ribbon about 1/2 inch from the end. Pull the long loose end of the ribbon until the ribbon slides up next to the eye of the needle, locking ribbon in place.

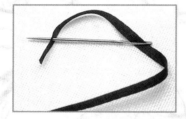

Figure 2: Spider Rose

For the spider rose, base stitch five even spokes that are anchored in the center of the circle (stitched here in blue for clarity). Work the spider rose by weaving the ribbon over and under the base threads. After the first time around, pull the ribbon so it covers the center of the base threads. Be sure to cover the anchor threads. To end, tuck the ribbon under the last row, pulling ribbon to the back side.

Figure 3: Lazy Daisy Leaf and Rosebud

Bring the needle up at 1; let the ribbon lie on top of the fabric, forming a loop. Holding the loop in place, go down at 2 right next to 1. Bring the needle up at 3, cross over the ribbon, going down at 4. Repeat for each lazy daisy.

Figure 4: Bead Attachment

Bring your needle up at 1, slide the bead in place. Go down at 2 and come up at 1. Slide the needle/thread back through hole of bead, going back down at 2. Pull your thread taut. Continue in this manner until all beads are placed.

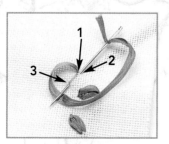

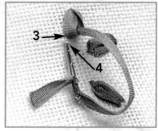
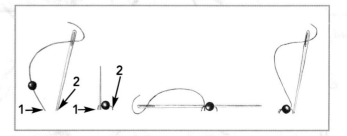

1 Cut an 8-by-10-inch piece of crushed fabric, interfacing, and batting. Set aside.

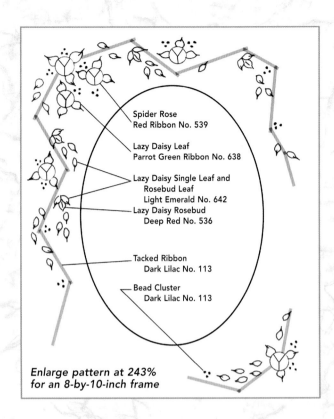

Spider Rose
Red Ribbon No. 539

Lazy Daisy Leaf
Parrot Green Ribbon No. 638

Lazy Daisy Single Leaf and
Rosebud Leaf
Light Emerald No. 642

Lazy Daisy Rosebud
Deep Red No. 536

Tacked Ribbon
Dark Lilac No. 113

Bead Cluster
Dark Lilac No. 113

Enlarge pattern at 243% for an 8-by-10-inch frame

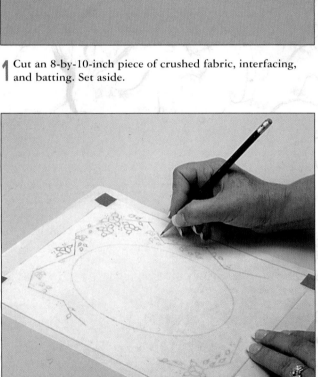

2 Trace the pattern onto the tracing paper using a permanent pen. Turn the traced pattern over so that the three spider roses are in the upper right corner to give you a mirror image. Center the piece of interfacing over the traced pattern with the fusible side next to the paper. Use the mechanical pencil to transfer the pattern onto the interfacing. Following fusible directions, iron interfacing to the back side of the crushed fabric.

3 HINT: To begin or end thread, run the needle between the interfacing and fabric back making sure it does not show on the front side.

Baste the traced pattern onto the fabric front using one strand of embroidery floss. Use No. 666 red floss to baste around the spider rose circle; do not put in the spokes. Use the red floss to place a straight stitch down the middle of the rosebuds and use No. 702 kelly green floss for the leaves. Use No. 553 violet floss, to place a long straight stitch the length of each section of the tacked ribbon and to make tiny stitches for the beads.

4 Work the spokes of the spider rose (Fig. 2) with No. 666 red floss. Weave in and out of the spokes with No. 539 red ribbon. Work the rose leaves with the lazy daisy (Fig. 3) using No. 638 parrot green ribbon. Come up under the edge of the spider rose being careful not to pierce the red ribbon.

Work the single leaves and rosebud leaves with the lazy daisy (Fig. 3) using No. 642 light emerald ribbon. Work the rosebuds with the lazy daisy using No. 536 deep red.

Using the iron, press lengths of No. 113 dark lilac ribbon for the tacked ribbon sections.

To lay the tacked ribbon, bring the needle/ribbon up from the back side under the edge of the spider rose/leaf, as indicated on the pattern. Lay the ribbon along each section of basting thread. Take the needle/ribbon down at the end of each section. Come back up in the middle and slightly over from the end of the previously laid ribbon. Repeat this until all sections are completed. Keep tacked ribbon as flat and smooth as possible. Refer to the photograph. Attach the beads (Fig. 4) over the tiny basting stitches using one strand of violet floss. Be sure the beads are secure.

5 Using Tacky Glue, secure the piece of batting to the mat and let dry. Trim away the batting in the center oval of the mat and trim edges as necessary.

Center the stitched fabric on the mat, and pin. Secure the four corners by folding the corner point of the fabric toward the center of the mat. Carefully pull the outside edges of the fabric around to the back of the mat bringing the two outer edges of the fabric together. (Be sure the front side is smooth and that the embroidery is still centered.) Use painter's tape to hold it in place. Trim edges as necessary.

Working from the back side, clip the fabric in the center oval, cutting toward the oval edge. Be careful not to cut too close to the mat.

Pull the fabric to the back side of the frame. Trim as needed and tape in place. When the fabric is smooth on the front, and the corners and sides are in place, remove one piece of tape at a time and glue fabric to the mat. HINT: Use a toothpick to place a small amount of glue under the edges of the fabric as you remove the tape.

Center the photograph on the easel back.

Before securing the easel back to the mat, trim the easel back flap so that the flap is even with the bottom and side of the easel back. Secure the mat to the easel back along the outer edges of the sides and bottom. The top edge of the easel is left open.

A Wrap for *Fall*

This elegant cross-stitched and stenciled candle decoration makes a lovely home accent.

This candle wrap is the perfect added touch for the coffee table when guests arrive for a special fall evening.

1 Find the center of the banding by folding it in half. Mark the center with a pin. Center the stencil horizontally and vertically on the banding, and tape in place with masking tape.

Read the directions that come with the paint before stenciling. We followed the directions for fabric, except we did not wash the banding. (The sizing on the fabric will keep the banding stiff.)

When stenciling, always begin with the lightest paint and end with the darkest.

Place the banding/stencil on a paper towel on a clean flat surface. When you are ready to stencil, mentally divide the paper plate in thirds using a third for each color. We used orange, green, and yellow stencil paint for the maple leaf.

Load your brush with a small amount of yellow paint and tap it up and down once or twice on the sheet of paper.

Using the same tapping motion, work around the maple leaf on the stencil, leaving a small section in the center unpainted. Load the same brush with green paint (tap on paper) and tap lightly in the leaf center, going over some of the yellow on the bottom area. TIP: If you're using only one brush, clean it by tapping on a paper towel. Do not use water!

For the oak leaf, we used orange and green paint. Load your brush with orange paint (tap on paper) and apply lightly. Load your brush with green (tap on paper) and tap over some of the orange along the leaf tips, bringing the paint into the center, but leaving some of the tips orange.

Set banding aside and let dry. TIP: Use straight pins and a wire coat hanger to secure the banding and make sure it doesn't touch anything as it dries.

You Will Need

- One 10½-inch piece, white, 28-count banding*
- Leaf stencil, stencil paint, and brushes**
- Masking tape
- Paper towels
- Paper plate and white sheet of typing paper
- Blending filament***
- Variegated six-stranded embroidery floss****
- No. 24 tapestry and embroidery needles
- 32 inches of ⅛-inch wide white double-faced satin ribbon
- White sewing thread
- Iron, scissors, general sewing supplies

*We used Charland 3½-inch wide banding (www.stitchville.com).

**We used American Traditional Leaves Medium Stainless No.SBM-031 stencil, 5-Piece Earthtone Set No. PS-400 Stencil Paint, No. B-4B and No. B-5B Stencil Brushes (www.AmericanTraditional.com).

***We used Kreinik No. 021 copper Blending Filament (www.kreinik.com).

****We used DMC Six-stranded Embroidery Mahogany Variegated Floss No. 111 and Avocado Green Lt. No. 470 (www.dmc-usa.com).

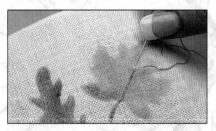 

2 EMBELLISHING: Use one strand of No. 470 floss with the stem stitch (Fig. 1) to work a center vein on each leaf. Work a few small veins going out from the center vein. TIP: To keep the blending filament from sliding out of the eye of the needle, use a very small knot to tie it to the eye.

Figure 1

SPECIAL SAFETY NOTE

These candle wraps should only be used with pillar candles, and, if you plan to light the candles, it's a good idea to remove the wrap to keep wax from dripping on it.

3 Use one strand of the No. 111 floss and No. 021 blending filament to work the cross-stitch (Fig. 2) for the top and bottom border. Center the border between the edge of the banding and the stenciled leaves. Start stitching on the left side, working across the band. Stitch the top line of cross-stitches and center line following the pattern, working across the band.

Figure 2

As you work across the band, run your thread under the center three stitches to be in position to work the next bottom three stitches. By working the pattern this way, it will keep your back threads from showing on the front side.

Return to the left side of the band to stitch the lower line of three cross-stitches.

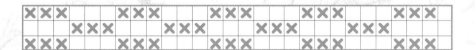

4 When stitching is completed, measure the circumference of your selected candle. Fold under the extra fabric on each end toward the back side of the banding. Pin in place. Place the banding around the candle, being sure the ends do not overlap. Using white sewing thread, slipstitch the folded edges to the back side of the band.

Cut four pieces of ribbon each 7 inches long. Pin the pieces of ribbon to the back side of the folded edge ½ inch from the top and bottom edges on both ends of the band, making sure the ribbons line up correctly. The top and bottom of each side of the banding should be level when tied. Use the white thread to secure the ribbons on the banding.

Place the finished band on the candle slightly below the center and tie in place to secure.

A Cozy *Winter*

This simple knitting project does double-duty—use the same instructions to create this afghan, or a simple scarf.

Snuggle in comfort this winter with a cozy afghan blanket that you can knit in this easy-skill-level project. Or if you like, knit a simpler project with the same instructions and make a luxurious scarf.

The pattern below shows instructions for the scarf, which measures 9 by 60 inches, with changes for the afghan (31 by 52 inches) noted in parentheses. When only one number appears, the instructions apply to both projects.

SPECIAL PROJECT TIP

The pattern below is written for the scarf with changes for the blanket in parentheses. When only one number is given, it applies to both pieces. Yarn colors (A, B, C, etc.) are shown in the "You Will Need" section. To follow the pattern more easily for the project you're creating, circle all the numbers that pertain to your piece before beginning.

You Will Need

- Size 10.5 [6.5 mm] knitting needles or size to obtain gauge
- One skein Homespun No. 378 Olive or color of your choice (A)
- One ball (two for blanket) Moonlight Mohair No. 206 Purple Mountain or color of your choice (B)
- Five balls (11 for blanket) Landscapes No. 277 Country Sunset or color of your choice (C)
- One ball Lion Suede No. 205 Waterlilies or color of your choice (D)

Note: All yarns are manufactured by Lion Brand (www.lionbrand.com). Homespun is packaged in 6-ounce [185 yard] skeins; Moonlight Mohair is packaged in 1¾-ounce [82 yard] balls; Landscapes is packaged in 1¾-ounce [55 yard] balls, and Lion Suede solid colors are packaged in 3-ounce [122 yard] balls; prints are packaged in 2¾-ounce [111 yard] balls.

New to Knitting?

This easy knitting project can be created by beginning knitters with just a little experience. If you're new to knitting visit www.lionbrand.com for detailed general knitting instructions. Lion Brand is a large manufacturer of yarns and other knitting materials. They also offer detailed, step-by-step information for similar projects.

GAUGE

Each 12-st repeat = 2¾ inches in Pattern st with C.
Be sure to check your gauge.

ABBREVIATIONS

k = knit
k2tog = knit 2 together
p = purl
st(s) = stitch(es)
tog = together

Stitch explanations

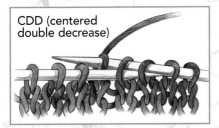

CDD (centered double decrease)

CDD (CENTERED DOUBLE DECREASE): Slip 2 sts as if to k2tog, knit next st, pass 2 slipped sts over.

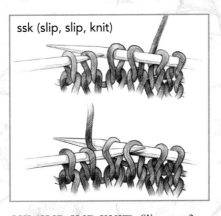

ssk (slip, slip, knit)

SSK (SLIP, SLIP, KNIT): Slip next 2 sts as if to knit, one at a time, to right needle; insert left needle into fronts of these 2 sts and k them tog.

PATTERN STITCH

Row 1 (right side): K 1, ssk, *k 9, CDD; repeat from * to last 12 sts, k 9, k2tog, k 1.

Row 2: K 1, *p 1, k 4, (k 1, yarn over, k 1) in next st, k 4; repeat from * to last 2 sts, p 1, k 1.

Repeat Rows 1-2 for Pattern st.

SCARF (BLANKET)

With A, cast on 39 (135) sts. Beginning with Row 1, work in Pattern st in the following Wide Stripe sequence: 2 rows A; 2 rows B; 4 rows C; 2 rows A; 2 rows B; 4 rows D; 2 rows A; 2 rows B.

Continue in Pattern st with C only for 9 (7) inches, ending with Row 2.

Then work in Pattern st in the following Narrow Stripe sequence: 2 rows B; 2 rows A; 4 rows D; 2 rows A; 2 rows B. Continue in Pattern st with C only for 10 (8) inches, ending with Row 2.

Work Wide Stripe sequence for 5½ inches.

Continue in Pattern st with C only for 10 (8) inches, ending with Row 2.

Work Narrow Stripe sequence for 3 inches.

Continue in Pattern st with C only for 9 (7) inches, ending with Row 2.

Work first 18 rows of Wide Stripe sequence (ending with 2 rows A).

Bind off with A as if to purl.

Needlepoint *Pillow*

Use this geometric design as the focal point of a decorative throw pillow.

Thishis unique, attractive design will catch anyone's eye as the center of a cute pillow.

It's a good idea to read through all of the following information before you begin this project.

You Will Need

- 8-by-8-inch 14-count white Interlock canvas *
- Masking tape
- 8-by-8-inch stretcher bars
- Thumbtacks
- No. 5 Pearl Cotton**
- No. 22 tapestry needles
- Six-stranded cotton floss
- Ecru sewing thread
- Embroidery needle
- Ecru trim***
- Scissors, ruler, straight pins, pencil, and general sewing supplies
- Fabric for pillow shell OR prepurchased pillow cover

- 14-by-14-inch pillow insert****
Optional:
- Fringe or other decorative accents

*We used Zweigart canvas (www.zweigart.com).
**We used DMC No. 5 Pearl Cotton: Ecru, No. 703 Chartreuse, No. 995 Electric Blue Dk. and DMC six-stranded floss No. 703 (www.dmc-usa.com).
***We used Europa Imports SKU No. 7162381.
****We used a Fairfield Soft Touch pillow insert (www.poly-fil.com).*

Special Information

It helps to read all instructions before starting to stitch.

The pattern and stitch graphs are very important in needlepoint. The pattern shows you where the stitch is placed in each section, and the graphs show you how the stitch is worked.

When working needlepoint, you count the threads so that you can be sure you work each stitch over the number of threads indicated on both the pattern and stitch graph. Always count and then recount to be sure you are correct.

Begin stitching using an away waste knot. Tie a knot in your thread and move 1 or 2 inches away in line with the stitching area. Put the needle down through the front of the canvas, coming up from the back side at your starting point. When you reach the knot, simply clip it off, and continue stitching. End the thread by running it under several previously worked stitches.

For the darning stitch, begin and end your thread in the reverse scotch stitch, running the thread under several stitches and coming out where you are to begin stitching. End the same way.

Note: Work in Sections

This design is worked in eight sections that border the center motif. You will work one section at a time, working all four sides of a section. Starting your stitching with the outer section of reverse scotch, work each section inward, toward the center motif area.

After the eight sections are worked, you will work the center motif area. The instructions will indicate which sections are to be worked with a given stitch and with the color of pearl cotton used.

It is important to follow the pattern and to have the stitches worked correctly by following the arrows and numbers on each stitch graph. If the stitches are worked correctly, there should be no back threads visible from the front.

1 Apply masking tape to the edges of the canvas. Secure the canvas to the stretcher frame with tacks or staples. Place 16 tacks or staples following Fig. 1 at right. Canvas should be firm to the touch and the threads should be straight. (This will ensure that the finished canvas is straight when removed from the frame.)

Use a pencil or pen to mark a 'T' on the tape at the very top of your canvas. This will help you keep all stitches going in the correct direction.

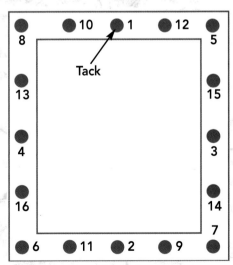

Figure 1

To Begin Stitching

Find the horizontal center of the canvas; count down eight threads from the bottom edge of the top stretcher bar. This will be your starting point for Section 1.

NOTE: The center of the pattern is indicated by a v at the top, bottom, and sides of the pattern.

Needlepoint Pillow

Enlarge pattern on a color copier at 210%

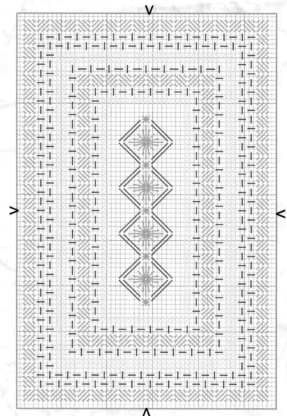

Color Key

Style	Number	Name
		ECRU
	703	Chartreuse
	995	Electric Blue Dk

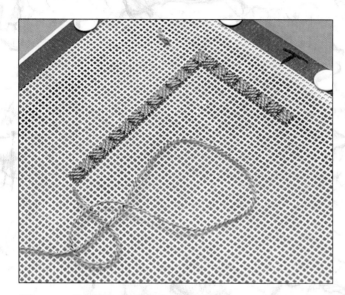

Figure 2: Sections 1 and 6— Reverse Scotch

Use No. 703 Chartreuse pearl cotton to work the reverse scotch for these sections. Start in the center (center indicated on pattern with a 'V') working to the left, around the area. You will notice on Fig. 2 after a stitch (square) is completed, it changes direction. It is important to follow the arrows/numbers, stitching in the direction indicated. Complete the section on all four sides, keeping your tension even as you work.

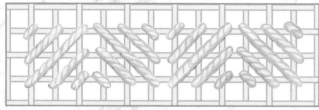

Figure 2: Reverse scotch

Figure 3: Sections 2, 3, 5, and 7—Two-Way Pattern Darning Variation

Use No. 995 Electric Blue Dk pearl cotton and the two-way darning variation for these sections. Begin and end your thread in the scotch stitch. Start on the upper left side just under the reverse scotch. You will work a vertical stitch, then a horizontal stitch, continuing in this manner following the pattern and stitch graph around the section. Do not pull your stitches too tightly or they will disappear into the canvas or become crooked.

For Section 3, you will start the thread in the reverse scotch and bring it down behind Section 2, starting with the vertical stitch in the upper left corner. Work Sections 3 and 7 in the same manner as Section 2.

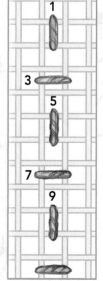

Figure 3

Figures 4 and 5:
Sections 4 and 8 use the Slanted Gobelin

Use Ecru pearl cotton to work these sections using the Slanted Gobelin stitch. For Section 4, the stitch is worked over three threads (Fig. 4) and for Section 8 it is worked over two threads (Fig. 5). The Slanted Gobelin is worked in the same manner whether it is over two or three threads. Start in the upper right corner, working around the area. You will be compensating in the upper left and lower right corners as you work around these sections. The need for a compensating stitch occurs when the indicated stitch does not fit into a given area. In this case the Slanted Gobelin does not fill the area. You will need to fit the stitch into the area by working several stitches of different lengths. Carefully follow the pattern when working the upper left and lower right corners. For this stitch, the needle enters the canvas at a different point as you go around the

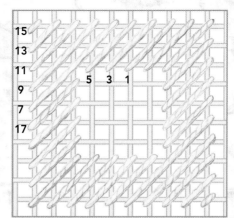

Figure 4: Slanted Gobelin Over 3

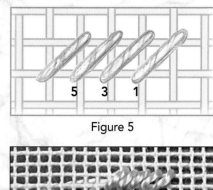

Figure 5

corners of the section, so be sure to change the stitch direction according to the stitch graph Fig. 4. When working Section 8, these two opposite corners will need a small stitch over one canvas thread as indicated on the pattern as you turn the corner.

Figures 6, 7, and 8:
Center Motif Area

Work the Smyrna Cross (Fig. 6) and the Algerian Eyelet (Fig. 7) using No. 995 Electric Blue Dk pearl cotton. Use an away waste knot in the path that you will travel. Start at the top in the center area as indicated on the pattern with a Smyrna Cross, then work the Algerian Eyelet, working vertically down the center motif as indicated on the pattern.

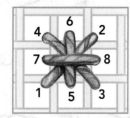

Figure 6: Smyrna Cross

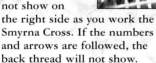

Be sure your thread does not show on the right side as you work the Smyrna Cross. If the numbers and arrows are followed, the back thread will not show.

Work the Diagonal stitch (Fig. 8) on each side of the center motif. Use No. 703 Chartreuse pearl cotton. Begin your stitching with an away waste knot placed outside the stitching area. It is important to count these stitches correctly and place the two diagonal stitches as indicated on the stitch graph. Refer to the pattern for placement of the first diagonal stitch. When stitching is completed, run your thread over and under the long threads just placed. Tie off your thread, being sure it does not show on the front side. Clip the waste knot, securing in the same manner.

Figure 7: Algerian Eyelet

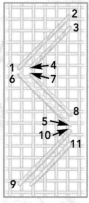

Figure 8:
Diagonal Stitch

Attaching the Needlepoint

Trim around the finished needlepoint, leaving three blank canvas threads on all sides. Pin the ecru trim along the outside edge to cover the three lines of blank canvas. Using ecru sewing thread, tack the trim over the blank canvas threads. Match trim at the end to hide where it joins. Trim outer canvas thread if necessary.

Center finished needlepoint in upper left corner of pillow cover (see photo), and secure with pins. Tack the piece in place, using one strand of No. 703 floss, carefully placing your stitches between the trim and scotch stitch. Use the ecru thread and a running stitch to hold needlepoint to the cover, being careful to hide stitches in trim.

A Kitchen *Garden*

Create an elegant cross-stitch towel with an herb motif.

As spring arrives the flowers start blooming. This cross-stitch design will bloom forever on your kitchen towels and potholders. We used this design for a towel and potholder but you can use it on any item you wish to embellish. The design can be used on a purse, book cover, sweater, tote bag, or even a small pillow.

You Will Need

- Towel and potholder with a cross-stitch insert*
- Embroidery floss**
- Tapestry needles No. 22 or 24
- Light-colored sewing thread for basting
- Scissors and general sewing supplies

The finished design for this project is: 54 squares wide by 70 squares high or 3½-by-3⅛ inches

*We used a Charles Craft Huck Towel in ecru style No. HF-6500-2724 and a KitchenMates Potholder, in ecru style No. PH-601-2724, (800) 277-0980 (www.charlescraft.com).

**We used DMC floss in very dark shell pink No. 221; medium pistachio No. 320; very dark blue violet No. 333; medium blue violet No. 340; light blue violet No. 341; dark pistachio No. 367; light pistachio No. 368; light tangerine No. 742; dark cornflower blue No. 792; medium baby green No. 966; dark blue violet No. 3746; very light blue violet No. 3747 and very dark old gold No. 3829 (www.dmc-usa.com).

Cross-Stitch Basics

Whatever uses you have for this design, remember these tips:
- Be sure your design is in the center of your fabric.
- Use 16- to 18-inch thread lengths.
- Separate the thread by holding the strand near the top of the cut length. With your other hand, pull one strand straight up and away from the hand holding the thread. Remove the strands needed and join them together again.
- To begin stitching, tie a knot in the end of the thread. Go about 2 inches over on the row where the first stitch will be placed. Take the needle down through the front side of the fabric; bring the needle up from the back side to the lower left corner of the first stitch. When the stitching reaches the knot, clip the knot and continue to stitch. To end threads, slip the needle/thread under several stitches on the back side.
- Remove basting thread as you work the cross-stitches.

How to Center the Design

Find the horizontal center of your fabric and run a basting thread across the area. Find the vertical center of the fabric and run a basting thread.

Your starting point will be where the center vertical and horizontal threads cross.

Special Instructions

- Use two strands of floss for the cross-stitches and to backstitch the letters.

- Use one strand for the straight stitches for the flower stigmas.

How to Work the Cross-Stitch

Follow the cross-stitch diagram, starting in the left corner of the square. At the starting point, bring your needle and thread up for 1 and take the needle across the square and down at 2. Come up at 3, going down at 4. Work all cross-stitches in this manner.

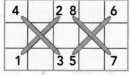

How to Work the Straight Stitches

Following the straight-stitch diagram, bring the needle up at 1; go across the area, going down at 2, being sure the threads lie flat as they go into the fabric. Come up at 3, go down at 4 and so on. Repeat as needed.

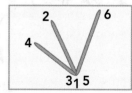

How to Work the Backstitch for the Lettering

Following the backstitch diagram, bring the needle up at 1; go across the square and down at 2, being sure the thread lies flat. Repeat this until the letters are completed. Come up at 3, go down at 4 and so on. Repeat.

DID YOU KNOW?

It takes more than 5,000 stigmas from approximately 1,700 Saffron crocuses to yield 1 ounce of the spice, dried saffron.

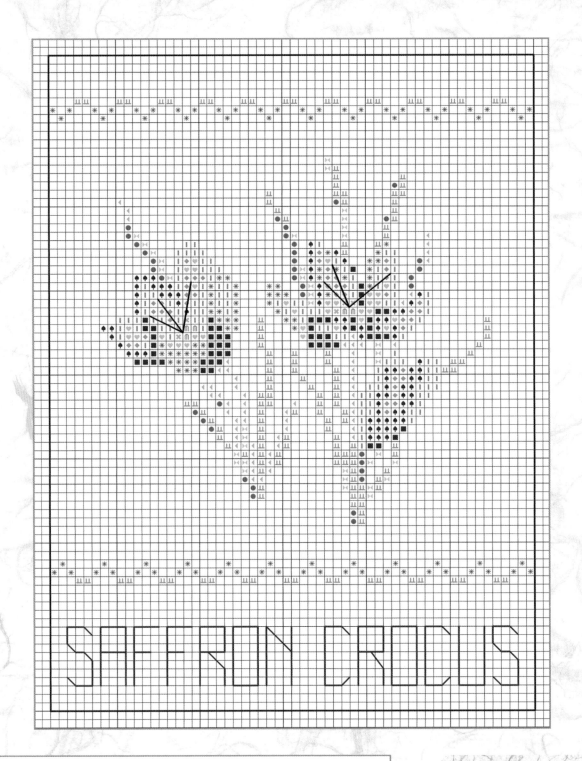

SAFFRON CROCUS

Color Key for Chart: Saffron Crocus

Symbol	Number	Name
⊥⊥	320	Pistachio Med
♠	333	Blue Violet VDk
I	340	Blue Violet Med
◆	341	Blue Violet Lt
●	367	Pistachio Dk
◄	368	Pistachio Lt

Symbol	Number	Name
✕	742	Tangerine Lt
■	792	Cornflr Blue Dk
⋈	966	Baby Green Med
✳	3746	Blue Violet Dk
♥	3747	Blue Violet VLt
⋔	3829	Old Gold Vy Dk

Style	Number	Name
——	221	Shell Pink V Dk - Straight Stitch
——	333	Blue Violet VDk - Backstitch

SPECIAL PROJECT TIPS

• When working with a potholder, place a piece of white paper inside the holder pocket. This keeps your needle from picking up the terry loops as you work the stitches.

• Also, when working with white cross-stitch fabric, lay a dark piece of fabric in your lap. It makes the spaces in the cross-stitch fabric easier to see.

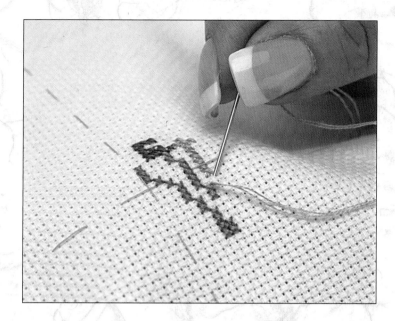

1 Following the cross-stitch chart and color key, start from the top left leaf of the crocus on the right—the center of the towel/potholder. Working on the right side of the basting thread, count upward four squares to start stitching at the top of the leaf, working just below the right flower. Complete the right flower and then work the left one.

2 Following the cross-stitch chart, place the straight stitches (No. 221 shell pink VDk) in the center of the flowers.

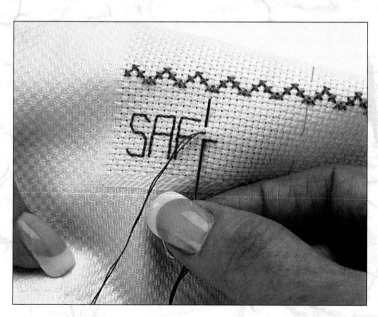

3 Following the cross-stitch chart, work the top and bottom border cross-stitches. Use the backstitch to work the lettering (No. 333 blue violet VDk) five squares below the bottom border and two squares over for the edge. You can travel with your thread as you work the letters.

   When ending thread, be careful not to disturb stitches on the front side.

Flowers in the *Bedroom*

Enjoy blooms inside all year with these silk ribbon pillowcases.

You Will Need

- Tracing paper
- Permanent pen or fine marker
- Pillowcases*
- Light box or sunny window
- Mechanical pencil
- No. 20 chenille needles
- Embroidery and beading needles
- Six-stranded cotton floss**
- Several colors of 4 mm silk embroidery ribbon ***

- Frosted glass beads****
- Sewing thread
- Iron, fluffy towel, straight pins, general sewing and crafting supplies

*We used Home 200-thread count pillowcases, purchased at Target.

**We used DMC Six-stranded Cotton Floss, No. 367 Pistachio Green Vy Lt. and No. 368 Pistachio Green Lt. (www.dmc-usa.com).

***We used 4 mm Bucilla Pure Silk Ribbon, No. 516 Dark Peach (2 cards), No. 565 Rose Red (3 cards), and No. 642 Light Emerald (1 card) (www.plaidonline.com).

****We used Wichelt/Mill Hill Frosted Glass Beads No. 62042 Royal Purple.

Getting Started

If you will be doing this project on a cotton/poly blend pillowcase, you may need to prewash the cases before stitching. If you will be using 100-percent cotton cases, iron them before transferring the pattern so your surface is nice and flat.

After you've transferred your pattern (see instructions on page 53), here are a few general tips for working with silk ribbon:

Secure the ribbon (Fig. 1) in the chenille needle's eye.

To begin stitching, leave a loose inch of ribbon hanging on the back of your work. After the first stitch is placed, bring the needle/ribbon to the back side and pierce the loose tail with the needle. Pull the ribbon through the tail to secure. To end ribbon, run it under a couple of stitches and pierce to secure.

Use your thumb to keep the ribbon flat for the lazy daisy as it goes into the fabric. The secret of a beautiful stitch is keeping the ribbon flat as it comes from the back of the fabric and goes down into the fabric. Be sure the edges of the ribbon come together in the center; if they don't, your ribbon was twisted.

Do not carry your stranded floss or ribbon to another flower/leaf; instead, end the floss or ribbon and begin again.

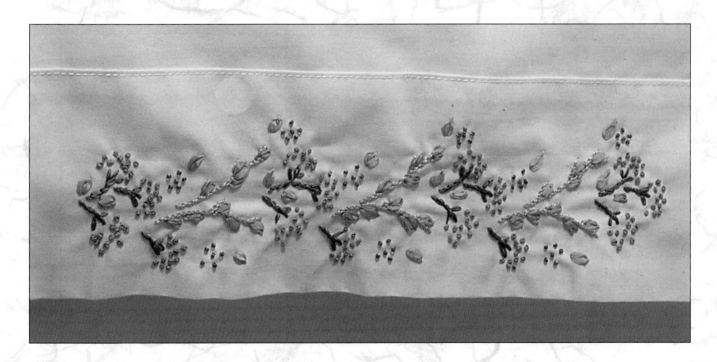

Threading the Needle

Use a 10- to 12-inch piece of ribbon; pull the ribbon through the eye about 3 inches. Pierce the ribbon about ½ inch from the end. Pull the long loose end of the ribbon until the ribbon slides up next to the eye of the needle, locking ribbon in place.

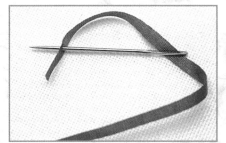

Figure 1

How to Work the Stem Stitch

Always keep the thread on the lower side of the needle, working the stem stitch along the traced line. Bring the needle up at 1 and down at 2. Needle comes up at 3 halfway between 1 and 2. Continue in this manner until area is completed.

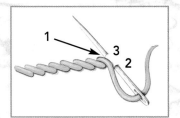

Figure 2

How to Work the French Knot

Bring the needle up at 1, turn the needle so it points toward your left arm. Wrap the ribbon once around the needle so it is not too snug. Hold the loose end of the ribbon with your opposite hand and turn the needle toward your heart and take the needle down into the fabric at 2. Let the loose ribbon you are holding slide through your fingers until it all goes to the back of the fabric. Continue in this manner until all the knots are in place.

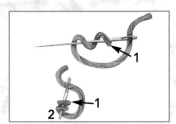

Figure 3

Lazy Daisy, Leaf, and Rosebud

Bring the needle up at 1; let the ribbon lie on top of the fabric forming a loop. Holding the loop in place, go down at 2 right next to 1. Bring the needle up at 3; cross over the ribbon, going down at 4. Repeat for each lazy daisy.

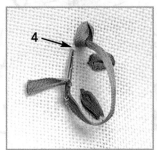

Figure 4

Beads

Bring your needle up at 1, slide the bead in place. Go down at 2 and come up at 1. Slide the needle/thread back through hole, going back down at 2. Pull your thread taut. Continue in this manner until all beads are placed.

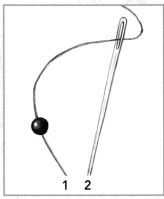

Figure 5

Style at Home

Step 1: Transferring the Pattern

Join two pieces of tracing paper with clear tape. Starting on the right side of your paper, trace the pattern onto the tracing paper using a permanent pen. The pattern is repeated three times across the border of the pillowcase. To repeat, overlap the last group of three French knot flowers with the three on the traced design. (Refer to the photo for the repeat of the pattern.)

Trim the paper so that it fits inside your pillowcase. Center the design horizontally and vertically on the border of the pillowcase. Have the design slightly closer to the folded bottom edge of the pillowcase. If it is too close to the stitched border edge, you will have to work through four pieces of fabric.

When the design is centered, pin in place. Move the bottom piece of the pillowcase out of the way so light comes through. Using a mechanical pencil and light box or sunny window, transfer the pattern onto your pillowcase.

TIP: To transfer the design, use a straight line for the detached leaves and a small dot for the beads indicated by small squares on the pattern. Make a small dot for the French knot flowers. It is not necessary to mark the rosebuds on the branches; you will fit the lazy daisy between the branch and stem.

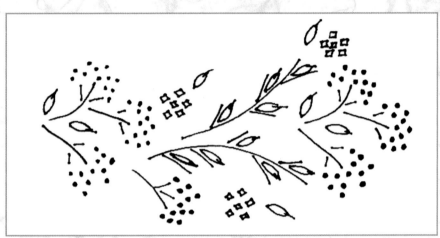

To use the pattern (left), photocopy at 137 percent. Trace and repeat the pattern three times along your pillowcase border.

Step 2: Working the Embroidery

Start stitching on the left side of the pillowcase. Use the stem stitch (Fig. 2) to work the stems of the three flowers using three strands of No. 367 stranded floss. Work the French knots (Fig. 3) of the flowers using No. 565 red rose ribbon, wrapping the ribbon around the needle one time. (NOTE: Use loose tension to keep stitches from puckering the pillowcase fabric. It is easy to pull your work too tightly when working with two layers of fabric.)

Using the lazy daisy (Fig. 4), work the detached leaves using No. 642 light emerald ribbon.

Using the stem stitch (Fig. 2), work the stems of the branches using three strands of No. 368 stranded floss. Using the lazy daisy (Fig. 4), work the buds on the branches using No. 516 light peach ribbon.

Using sewing thread, attach the beads (Fig. 5) over the small groups of six dots. Sew through each bead twice to secure.

Continue working toward the right, repeating until the border is complete.

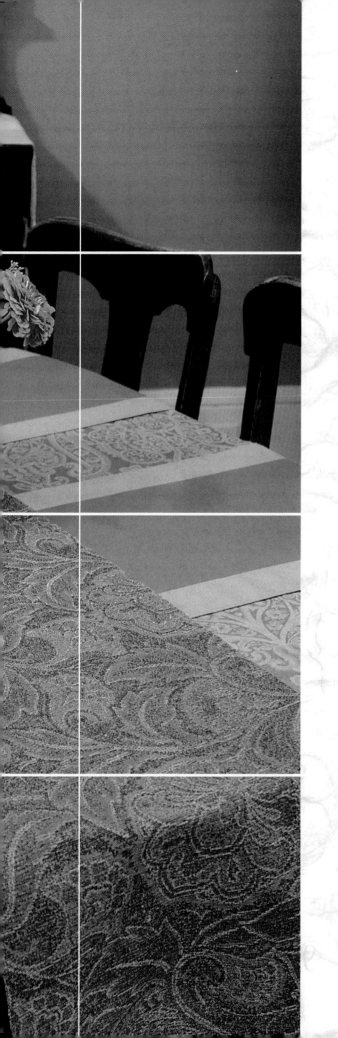

Sewing
with *Style*

These distinctive projects range from sewing with vintage linens and creating a classic floppy bunny ... to making a clever beach bag or a blanket from second-hand suits. Fabric selections galore let you follow your heart to a style that fits you just right.

Vintage *Style*

Transform old linens into a perfect new bed ensemble.

Vintage linens tend to be exceptionally decorative, with attractive embroidery, unique cutwork, and other clever details.

All too often, these pieces seldom escape the drawers in which they reside. Why not showcase the handiwork that went into these items?

This project turns a lavishly embroidered dresser scarf into a decorative bed bolster. The dresser scarf is applied to the front of a sewn bed bolster and used to anchor a collection of decorative pillows that also feature other unique old-time linens.

This project may also spark your own creativity. Why not turn delicate old hand towels into throw pillows, or spotlight delicate cutwork by reusing the piece as part of a pillow sham? The possibilities are endless.

Getting Started

Measure the length and circumference of your bolster form and add 1 inch to each measurement. Cut a rectangle from your decorative fabric equal to these measurements. (NOTE: The dresser scarf you use should be smaller, widthwise, than the cut piece of decorative fabric.)

Measure the width of the end of your bolster and add 1 inch. Cut two circles of decorative fabric equal to this measurement. These will form the ends of the bolster. (TIP: Use a large bowl or a plate to make a circular pattern.)

All seam allowances are ½ inch unless otherwise specified.

SPECIAL PROJECT TIP

To finish our bed ensemble, we stitched two decorative pieces of cutwork to the outside front of two other decorative bed pillows we made. We also created a geometric pillow to complement the fabrics on the bed.

1 Cut decorative fabric as noted in Getting Started above.

Press dresser scarf. Center scarf in the middle of the cut decorative fabric rectangle and pin in place. Topstitch all four sides of the scarf to the fabric, keeping your stitches as close to the decorative edges as possible.

2 Welting adds a nice finished edge to this piece. If you decide not to add welting to your bolster, skip to Step 4.

Cut two strips of decorative fabric on the bias for the welting. For our bolster, we cut a piece of fabric 2 inches wide by 28 inches long. Install the zipper foot on your sewing machine. With wrong sides together, wrap the bias strip around your welting cord and stitch, keeping your stitches as close to the cord as possible.

3 With right sides together, align the raw edge of the cording with the outside edge of the sides of the decorative fabric and pin. TIP: Keep the heads of the pins toward you so they can be easily removed as you sew. Stitch cording in place, keeping stitches as close to the corded edge as possible.

4 With right sides together, fold decorative fabric in half along the length. Machine stitch to within 4 inches from the end, leaving a large opening which will be used to insert the bolster form.

5 With right sides together, pin circles to each end of the bolster. Sew in place, keeping your stitches as close to the corded edge as possible. Clip the curved edge, being careful not to clip through stitching. Turn bolster right side out, press, and insert the pillow form. Hand sew opening closed.

The Velveteen Rabbit

Say "welcome!" to spring with the floppy-eared charm of these classic bunnies.

Baby bunnies are always irresistible, and these fuzzy friends are no exception.

Using the simple pattern provided below, you can create these cute critters by the crateful to provide a wonderful gift for yourself or a friend.

You Will Need

- 1 yard bunny body fabric (we used low-nap velvet)
- Matching thread
- Small piece of remnant fabric for contrasting ears
- Scissors
- Wonder Under fusible webbing
- Fiberfill
- Embroidery thread in black and pink, and needle
- Sewing and curved needles
- Ready-made doll clothes and accessories*
- Ribbon and ribbon rosettes

We found the pink and green crocheted dress at our local Michael's store. The purse is actually a Christmas ornament that we used to add a fun note to our little girl bunny.

Getting Started

Cut all pattern pieces, and leave attached to fabric until you are ready to sew them. All seam allowances are ¼ inch unless otherwise specified.

Clip seam allowances at all curved areas, being careful not to clip through sewn seam. This will help all curved areas to lie flat.

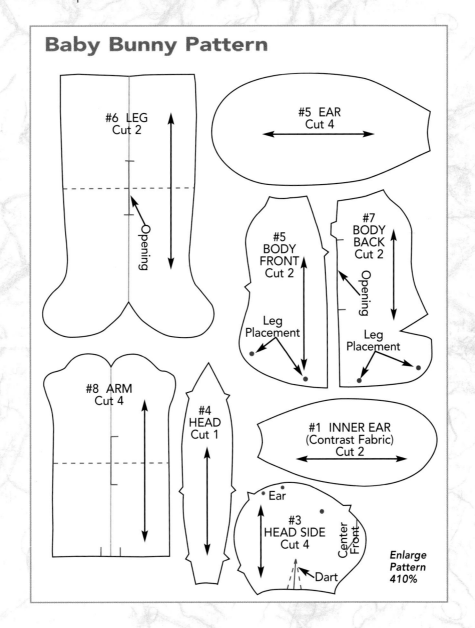

Baby Bunny Pattern

#6 LEG
Cut 2

Opening

#5 EAR
Cut 4

#5 BODY FRONT
Cut 2

#7 BODY BACK
Cut 2

Opening

Leg Placement

Leg Placement

#8 ARM
Cut 4

#4 HEAD
Cut 1

#1 INNER EAR
(Contrast Fabric)
Cut 2

Ear

#3 HEAD SIDE
Cut 4

Center Front

Dart

Enlarge Pattern 410%

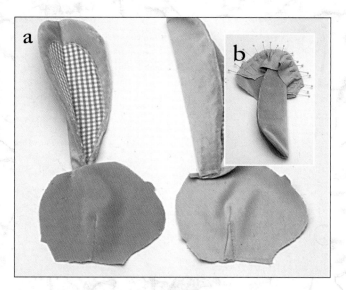

1 FOR THE EAR AND CONTRASTING INNER EAR: Iron Wonder Under to wrong side of contrasting inner ear following manufacturer's instructions. Place inner ear piece over right side of ear. Center and line up the bottom edges. Fuse in place.

Satin stitch along raw outside edge of inner ear fabric. Pin two ear pieces right sides together and stitch in place, leaving bottom edge open. Turn ear right side out and press. Repeat with the other ear.

Fold ear in half (contrasting fabric to inside), and stitch along bottom edge. Repeat with other ear.

2 MAKING THE HEAD: Sew a small dart in the head sides at markings. Press dart toward the back of the head. Pin the ear to the head side, right sides together and baste in place.

Pin the center piece of the head to one of the sides, right sides together, lining up markings and sew in place up to square marking. Repeat on opposite side.

Stitch from lower edge opening to square marking on each side to complete the head. Turn right side out.

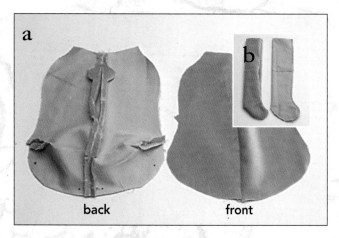

back   front

3 FOR THE BODY AND LEGS: With right sides together, pin and sew the body back pieces together, leaving a 3-inch opening in the center of the back for turning and stuffing (photo 3a). Sew darts in body back pieces.

With right sides together, sew the body front together.

Fold legs in half, right sides together. Pin and sew, leaving the top of the leg open as well as an opening in center of leg for stuffing (photo 3b).

Turn right side out and press.

With right sides together, pin legs to body front at markings. The toes should be facing toward the front of the body (photo 3c). Baste.

Pin front to back of body, right sides together, matching markings. Sew.

NOTE: Do not sew the opening at the neck and do not turn body right side out.

4 ATTACHING THE HEAD: Pin head to body, right sides together, matching marking and side seams (photo 4a).
TIP: Pull ears through the opening in the center back of the body. Sew.

NOTE: You'll find that it is easier to hand baste the head in place and then remove pins before sewing the head in place on your sewing machine.

Turn the head and body right side out. Firmly stuff the bunny with Fiberfill; starting with the head, then the body and legs (photo 4b).

Hand stitch opening on body and legs closed.

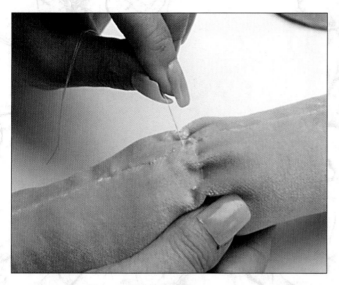

5 FOR THE LEG JOINT: Double thread a needle with coordinating colored thread. Run a basting stitch around the center of the leg. Pull thread tightly, gathering the fabric to create a joint.

6 FOR THE ARMS: Fold arms in half the same way you did the legs, right sides together. Pin and sew, leaving only the top open.

Turn right side out and press.

Firmly fill arms with fiberfill. Turn raw edges in at the top of the arms. Hand sew opening closed, gently pleating fabric as you sew the opening closed to create a soft round shape on the top of the arm.

Create joints in arms following instructions in Step 5.

Pin arms in position on the body with thumbs facing toward the front. Hand sew the arms into place, stitching from the underside of the arm to conceal stitches.

TIP: It helps to use a curved needle when attaching the arms.

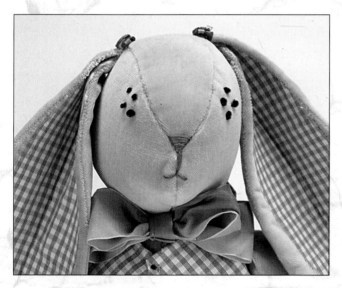

7 FINISHING TOUCHES: To create eyes, use 5 or 6 strands of black embroidery thread and embroider four French knots for each eye (Fig. 1). TIP: Use pins to determine location of eyes.

Using a satin stitch, create the nose and mouth using 3 to 4 strands of pink embroidery thread (Fig. 2).

Insert the needle at the center position where the head and sides of face meet. Create roughly six stitches toward the top of the head. Reinsert the needle down to the center position, and use one stay stitch for the upper mouth crease and two more stitches to create the mouth.

You can then add ribbons, ribbon rosettes, and ready-made doll clothes to give your bunny an individual personality.

How to Work the French Knot

Bring the needle up at 1, turning the needle so it points toward your left arm. Wrap the thread twice around the needle so it is snug but not tight. Hold the loose end of the thread with your opposite hand, turn the needle toward your heart, and take the needle down into the fabric near 1 but not in the exact same hole. Let the loose thread you are holding slide through your fingers until it all goes to the back of the fabric. Continue in this manner until all the knots are in place.

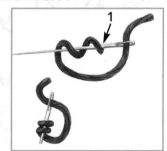

Figure 1

How to Work the Satin Stitch

Bring the needle up at 1 and go across the area, going down at 2. Bring the needle back up at 3 next to 1. Go back across the area, going down next to 2. Continue working the area in this manner.

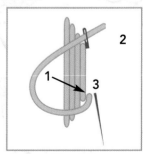

Figure 2

Beach Bag *Boogie*

It's a bag—or a bag AND a blanket! Turn any beach towel into an easy carryall that promises versatile summer fun.

Finding a way to carry everything you need to the beach or to a picnic can be tough, so any timesavers are welcome.

In these two projects, we found a way to turn a colorful beach towel into a clever—and spacious!—tote. In the second version of this project, we were able to create a tote that also unhooks easily, reverting to a beach towel that will let you lounge in comfort.

The materials for this project are inexpensive, and you can complete your tote in under two hours.

Beach Towel Bag

1 Working on the wrong side of the towel, pin bias tape 8½ inches down from the top edge of the towel and 3 inches in from the side on each edge. Repeat on the opposite end of the towel. Sew bias tape in place keeping the stitches as close to the outside edges of the tape as possible.

2 Fold towel in half, wrong sides together, along the length, lining up the top and bottom edges as well as the sides. Measure down 8 inches on each side of the towel and mark this measurement with a pin. Insert additional pins along the sides to keep edges lined up.

In order to create a 2½-inch sewing guide on your machine, place a piece of tape 2½ inches out from needle. Sew sides closed starting below the 8-inch pin marking, lining up the edge of the towel with the inside edge of the tape.

3 Turn down top edges of the towel 7 inches, exposing the wrong side of the towel. Pin in place on all four corners to keep turned edge in place (photo 3a).

Cut two pieces of nylon strapping 33 inches long. TIP: Before pinning the strapping to the towel, you can use a lighter to carefully melt the edge of the nylon strapping to avoid any fraying.

To create a carrying strap on the bag, pin strapping 2 inches down and 1 inch in from outside edge on each side of the towel, pinning through two layers of towel only. NOTE: The strapping and the towel will be too thick to sew through four layers of towel and strapping at the same time. Sew strapping in place (photo 3b).

4 Cut two pieces of nylon cord equal to the width of the towel plus 12 inches. Secure the cord to the safety pin. Push the safety pin through the bias tape until it reaches the opposite side of the towel. Repeat on the opposite side.

5 Run the cord through the toggle and knot each end of the cord. The toggles will now secure the closure of the beach bag.

Bag/Beach Blanket

With this project variation, your beach bag can double as a bag or a towel.

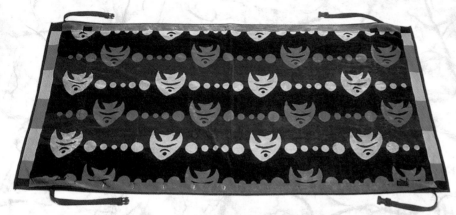

The unfolded bag (left) still works as a beach towel; the rebuttoned bag (above) is ready to carry all your gear home.

You Will Need

The elements from the previous project, plus:

- Fabric marking pencil
- Twelve 1-inch buttons
- Two interlocking plastic clasps

Getting Started

Follow instructions in Step 1 on page 63 for Beach Towel Bag before beginning Step 1 for this project.

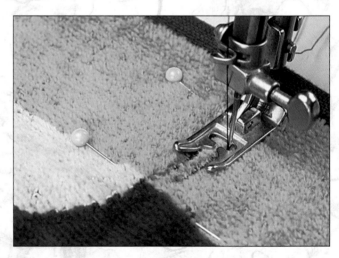

1 Follow instructions in Step 1 on page 63 for the Beach Towel Bag before proceeding with the rest of this step.

Fold towel in half wrong sides together along the length, lining up the top and bottom edges as well as the sides. Measure down 10 inches from the top edge of the towel and 2 inches up from the bottom folded edge of the towel and mark these measurements with a pin. (These are the placements for the first and last buttons.)

Measure the distance between these two markings and divide the measurement to equally space four more buttons. (Our buttons were about 5 inches apart. Mark the location for each button/buttonhole with a pin and/or marking pencil. Repeat on the opposite side.

2 NOTE: Markings for buttonholes are usually done with a marking pencil or chalk. On terrycloth, it's useful to use pins as your guide to mark the width of the buttonholes because it can be hard to make visible marks with a marking pencil on the towel.

The width of the buttonholes should be $\frac{1}{4}$ inch wider than the width of the buttons—our buttonholes were $1\frac{1}{4}$ inches wide. Insert pins vertically $1\frac{1}{4}$ inches apart at all the buttonhole markings starting 1 inch in from the outside edge of the towel.

Machine stitch all buttonholes.

Clip openings on all buttonholes, being careful not to clip through the stitching.

3 Fold towel in half along the length, lining up all edges. Mark button locations using pins or marking pencil. TIP: We found pushing a pin through the buttonhole was the easiest way to mark the location of the buttons.

Sew buttons at each marking. The center of each button should be about 1½ inches from the outside edge of the towel.

4 Unbutton towel. Measure down 7 inches from the top edge of the towel on each side and mark the location with a pin and/or marker. Repeat at opposite end of towel. Make a buttonhole at each marking 1¾ inches wide, following instructions in Step 2.

5 Cut 4 strips of nylon strapping 19 inches long. Run strapping through the clasps and sew in place (photo 4a). Pin strapping 8 inches down from top edge and 1 inch in from side edge of towel. Sew securely in place (photo 4b).

Push clasps through the buttonholes on each side of towel (photo 4c).

To finish your towel, follow the instructions on Step 4 and 5 of the beach towel bag on Page 63 (photo 4d).

Cuddle in *Comfort*

This fabulous flea market treasure creates a gorgeous winter throw out of men's old wool suits!

If you spend any time browsing through thrift shops or at flea markets, one item you'll find that often seems to go begging are old suits. These articles of clothing are often out of style, making them less apt to be snapped up by savvy shoppers.

However, these suits are a bargain if you look at them from the standpoint of quality materials. Tweeds, checks, and good wool are common and a single suit can easily contain more than three yards of material.

That inspired this project: We made use of those beautiful fabrics by cutting and piecing together an extra warm, luxurious throw. We also added a little whimsy to the project by keeping some of the suit's details, such as side pockets, and incorporating them into our final design. You'll find the pattern we used on page 68, but to save yourself a little time when creating this project, you can cut all your fabric squares the same size, if you like.

We made an extra-warm throw, lining our piece with a warm interlining and backing it with corduroy. You can make a lighter throw by omitting the interlining and backing your project with a thinner fabric.

Getting Started

Rip coats and pants apart using a seam ripper and scissors. NOTE: If you will be using the sections of the suit that contain pockets, sew all openings closed and cut off the actual interior part of the pockets.

Decide which fabrics will go where on your pattern layout (see page 68) to ensure that fabrics with similar details will not be next to each other after you sew them.

Cut out pattern pieces and number them. TIP: Keep pattern pieces pinned to the fabric until you are ready to sew them together.

All seam allowances are ½ inch unless specified otherwise.

You Will Need

- 4 or 5 used men's suits (dry clean or launder them before use)
- Paper for pattern (brown paper bags work well)
- Ruler or square
- Measuring tape
- Scissors
- Cutting mat and rotary cutter
- 5 yards of matching corduroy or other backing fabric
- Thread to match

Optional:
- 3 yards of cotton interlining*

Our interlining was made by The Warm Company and had a feel much like pressed felt. You can find this product at your local fabric store, or visit www.warmcompany.com.

Throw pattern

2 1/2 X 2 1/2 for all corner pieces

Finished Measurements

12 X 12	9 X 21	12 X 18
12 X 9		

6 X 12   10 X 12

16 X 9

49 X 2 1/2

12 X 6   9 X 6   12 X 9   16 X 6

22 X 9

9 X 18   12 X 12   6 X 15

70 X 2 1/2

12 X 12   12 X 6

10 X 18   6 X 6

21 X 12   6 X 9

12 X 15

10 X 9

12 X 9   15 X 6

8 X 3

14 X 7   12 X 4   8 X 4   15 X 7

70 X 2 1/2

Pattern at left represents *Finished Measurements* in inches. Add 1 inch in width and length to all pattern pieces to allow for 1/2-inch seam allowances.

Pattern: We decided to vary our throw by creating an interlocking system of different-shaped pieces of material. If you want to make a simpler throw, you can always make all of your pieces the same size, and simply sew them together that way.

SPECIAL PROJECT TIP

Some fabrics will tend to stretch more than others, so be very careful not to pull on pieces while sewing and pinning.

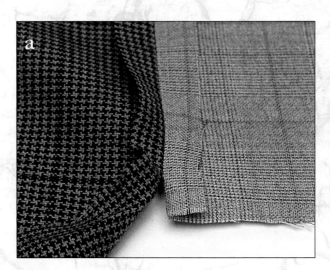

a

1 Sew pattern pieces right sides together, stopping 1/2 inch from end (photo 1a). (This will allow odd-sized squares and rectangles to line up properly along seams and finish corners, and this will also make sewing pieces together much easier.)

Sew pieces together following the pattern above. Press open all seams (photo 1b).

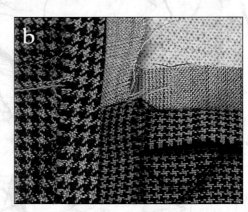

b

2 With right sides together, sew side strips to right and left side of throw. With right sides together, attach small squares to both ends of the top and bottom strips. With right sides together, pin strips to top and bottom of throw and sew. Press all seams open.

3 OPTIONAL: Place throw on interlining and cut interlining equal to the size of the throw.

Pin throw carefully to interlining, starting in the center and working your way toward the outside edges. Use several pins, making sure that all corners and seams are flat.

Topstitch inside all seams starting at center squares, working out toward edges.

4 Place throw over corduroy or backing fabric and cut backing fabric equal to the size of the throw.

With right sides together, pin throw to corduroy/backing fabric and sew, leaving an opening for turning.

Clip corners and turn right side out. Press, turning raw edges of opening in.

5 Hand stitch opening closed. Topstitch around entire throw ½ inch from outside edge.

Double *Duty*

These reversible table runners make any gathering a little more special. Plus, this one sewing project gives you several different looks.

Setting an inviting table is one way to make guests feel welcome. With Thanksgiving just around the corner, you might want to try your hand at these elegant reversible table runners in this simple sewing project.

One key to getting the most use out of these items is to select fabrics that complement each other. It's always a good idea to lay swatches of the fabrics you select on top of one another while you're still in the store. The fabrics don't need to match, but selecting colors in the same family of shades gives the most pleasing result.

We selected our fabrics from our local Hancock Fabrics store. They are an antique gold Kingswood Paisley decorative fabric by Waverly and light brown and gold Cape Cod linen (No. 971994 and No. 972059, respectively).

Getting Started

Measure the width and length of your table. Determine the finished width of the table runner as well as the desired drop length for the table runner. (Measure from the end of your table to the top of a chair seat.) Add twice the drop length to the width and length measurements.

Our table was 64 inches long and 42 inches wide. We decided that our finished width would be 16 inches and our drop length would be 10 inches. We also determined that the size of the banded edge would be 2½ inches on each side. (All seam allowances for this project are ½ inch unless otherwise specified.) The following cut measurements are for this measurement:

Table runner across the length of the table:
- Decorative/patterned fabric: Cut 1 strip 22 inches wide by 85 inches long
- Brown fabric: Cut 1 strip 12 inches wide by 85 inches long

Table runners across the width of the table:
- Gold fabric: Cut 1 strip 22 inches wide by 63 inches long
- Brown fabric: Cut 1 strip 12 inches wide by 63 inches long

You Will Need

- Decorative/patterned fabric (we used 2½ yards)*
- Plain fabric in two colors (we used 2½ yards of brown and 2 yards of gold)
- Measuring tape
- Large ruler
- Scissors
- Pins
- Heavy Duty Wonder Under Transfer Web by Pellon
- Matching thread

Optional:
- Decorative trim

*Your fabric requirements may vary depending on pattern repeat and table dimensions.

SPECIAL PROJECT TIP

Our decorative fabric had a beautiful leaf pattern that we decided to appliqué to our table runner. To do this, choose a fabric that has a pattern that can be cut out to create an appliqué. It adds a wonderful detail to the finished look of the table runner.

1 OPTIONAL APPLIQUÉ TECHNIQUE: Our decorative fabric had elegant leaf shapes in it. We decided to use these as a decorative appliqué for our center runner.

To do this, cut out several different sizes and shapes of a part of the pattern from your decorative fabric, leaving about ½ inch of additional fabric around the leaf.

Fuse Wonder Under to the wrong side of the leaf following manufacturer's instructions. Cut out the leaf and trim excess fabric on edge. Remove the paper backing and place randomly on brown fabric of table runner.

2 Set your sewing machine to satin stitch. Satin stitch around the outside edge of each leaf.

3 Pin the fabric strips together, aligning the raw edges on the long sides. Sew in place. Press seams open.

4 Lay runner on a flat surface. Measure 2½ inches from the seam to the outside edge of the fabric at one end of the runner and pin in place. Measure from the seam to the outside edge on the opposite side to ensure that the brown fabric is centered. Pin in place (photo 4a). Sew across the end of the runner. Clip corners and turn fabric right side out (photo 4b).

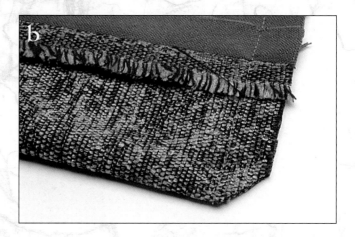

5 Lay runner on a flat surface. Starting on one side of the runner, measure 2½ inches from the seam to the outside edge along the entire length of the runner and pin in place, inserting the pins along the seam line. Repeat on the opposite side. Press outside edges. Press under ½ inch hem at unfinished end of runner and pin in place.

6 Topstitch along seam lines. Topstitch along outside edges, keeping stitching as close to edge as possible. (This will keep the edges of the table runner crisp and tailored.)

One More Idea

You can add an even more decorative aspect to any of these runners by fusing decorative trim in place over seam lines on both sides of the runner.

SPECIAL PROJECT TIP

Keeping sewing lines straight while topstitching along outside edges can be difficult. Place fabric in position on your sewing machine. Lay a long piece of tape along the outside edge of the fabric. This will now be your stitching guide.

Creative *Crafts*

Creativity doesn't have to be hard. Discover easy ways to dress up candles, blue jeans ... or your dinner table. You'll also find perfect gifts to make, like a creative bath and beauty set, a memorable shadowbox or a simple hand-woven bag. These simple crafts make style a cinch.

A Luxurious *Soak*

Tub-time never looked as good as it does with this decorative two-tiered bathroom shelf that holds oils and beauty supplies.

Finding a way to use familiar items in a unique way is always a pleasure. That was the case with this decorative two-tiered spice rack, a fun piece that seemed to offer more possibilities than simply as a kitchen item.

We decided to turn this rack into a "personal spa," complete with decorative details and a bevy of feel-good bath salts and other items that combine to make a perfect gift—whether it's for you or a friend.

You Will Need

- One two-shelf spice rack*
- Six glass spice jars
- Art Nouveau Initials**
- Scissors
- Computer
- Mod Podge matte sealer
- ¼-inch flat brush
- Acrylic rhinestones
- Thick craft glue
- Images for bottles and soaps***
- One sheet of 8-by-10-inch double-sided adhesive
- Cutting mat
- Craft knife
- Ruler
- Straight pin
- Six small flowers, your choice
- Long-nosed pliers w/wire cutters

*Our spice rack came from Gift Warehouse and sold for $13.99, plus S&H. No. 34352 (www.giftwarehouse.com).

**The alphabet letters we used come ready-to-use in a paperback book form for $6.95 from Dover Publications (www.doverpublications.com or look for this at your local craft store). You could also print out your initials on a computer in a fancy script and use those.

***We found our ready-made collage of images at www.artchixstudio.com. The sheet we used, called Wings of Fancy, No. C210, contains 13 images and sells for $5 a sheet, with discounts for multiple orders.

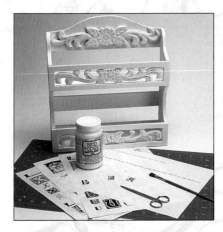

1 A number of companies make ready-to-photocopy lettering that can be used in a variety of projects. For this one, we photocopied ornate lettering that spelled out the word "Beauty." We cut out our letters, and then used a computer to print out two appropriate phrases for the lower front portions of our shelf. (You can add any sentiment you want to this project, such as the lines from a poem or other meaningful phrases.)

We glued our sentiments to our shelf, and then coated them with two coats of matte sealer, letting the material dry between applications.

2 We used several decorative vintage images from a company called Wings of Fancy to decorate our spice bottles. We applied double-stick adhesive to the backs of the images, and then cut them out with scissors. We then applied each image to our spice bottles, smoothing down in the center and working outward. (TIP: Use a straight pin to start the release paper).

3 Using a good quality craft glue, glue acrylic rhinestones on the front of the spice rack where you like. Let dry.

You'll find that you can purchase several combined stems of plaster flowers in the wedding section of your local craft store very inexpensively. Use a wire cutter to cut individual flowers from the flower bunches leaving a 1-inch stem on each one. Curl the stems. Screw the lids down on the glass spice jars, and then glue a single flower onto each jar lid facing toward the front of the jar. Let dry.

4 To finish your spa shelf, add a variety of special bath salts, oils, or creams to the spice jars. Finish the lower shelf with a few tied washcloths tucked inside. You can also purchase inexpensive bath soaps, wrap them in white tissue paper, and apply additional matching images from the spice jars to the soaps for an extra gift.

5 minutes for Candles
for Candles

Everybody loves how candles light up a room. Try these quick tips for changing plain candles into featured conversation pieces. (These candles make great gifts, but be sure to decorate extras for yourself.)

To help you enjoy your candles safely, remember these tips: Never leave any burning candle unattended. If you like the look of your fully decorated candles, you can leave them unburned as an accent item. If you plan to burn the candle, be aware that you may need to remove some of your embellishments to keep them from accidentally igniting.

TIP: If you want to burn a decorated pillar candle, consider letting it burn until there is a well about the size of a tea light inside the top. Then blow out the candle, snip off the wick on the pillar, and drop a tea light into the well. You can then burn the tea light instead of your art candle without sacrificing its appearance.

Dressed for Dinner

Jewelry and candles can be a delightful match. Consider embellishing taper candles, with their clean lines and sense of occasion. Add another visual element to these beauties by collecting a few old necklaces with rhinestones, beads, or shells, and then drape the necklaces around the base of the taper. You can reuse these necklaces again and again to add a sense of drama to a centerpiece. Or wrap a ribbon around your favorite candle, and then straighten the pin on the back of a decorative brooch and gently pin the piece onto the candle over the ribbon.

Art for the Office

This classy look is just too simple! Using a bag of simple office clasp fasteners, we snipped about two-thirds of the metal tab off each fastener with a wire cutter, leaving about a quarter inch of the tab on the head. (It may be easier to cut the tabs off at an angle, leaving yourself a point to press into your candle.)

With the tabs closed, press the fastener into the candle slowly. You can also try this with decorative snaps that are available in the scrapbooking sections of craft stores!

Say it with Candles

Scrapbook embellishments aren't just for paper anymore. These candle displays make lovely wedding or shower gifts. We used Metal Words from Making Memories for both these items.

For the candle at left, we used a package of Wire Words, which have a small loop of wire at each end. We secured the words to the candle with short appliqué pins. (You can also create your own words with wire writing kits available at craft stores.)

For the "forever" candle, we selected our word and gently formed it around the curve of the candle. We glued the word against the candle using Glue Lines, and then wrapped a length of ribbon around the piece to finish.

Shimmer and Shine

This quick and easy technique uses spray webbing or glitter. We used a spray webbing product by Krylon to spray several candles at one time for great last-minute gifts. (Be sure that you are using a spray box for this one and be aware that the webbing sprays in a random pattern; be sure you move your spray can evenly from side to side.) If you use glitter spray, try masking off one section of the candle with painter's tape for a clean look. You may spray your candles more than once to achieve the result you like.

Bounties of Beads

We used beading wire, assorted seed and bugle beads, and straight pins to make this elegant wrap. Simply cut a length of beading wire long enough to wrap around your candle several times, make a loop at one end of the wire to secure the beads, and thread the beads onto the wire. Twist a second loop at the end of the wire and trim close to the beads. Secure one loop to the candle with a pin, and wrap the candle with the beaded wire. Secure the second loop with another pin.

Chill *Chaser*

This cozy no-sew fleece poncho is perfect for snuggling through cool weather.

This no-sew poncho is cuddly, cute, and oh-so-simple to create.

In fact, this project is simple enough for tweens and teens to make. Take advantage of the gorgeous colors of fleece available in fabric stores, and mix that material with any type of colorful pony bead to give this project your own special touch.

You Will Need

- Fleece fabric*
- 6-inch ruler
- Scissors
- Straight pins
- Rotary cutter, cutting mat, and quilt ruler
- Two or more yards of ¼-inch satin picot ribbon*
- Craft knife
- Approximately 700 of 6-by-9mm opalescent white pony beads**
- Size 5 steel crochet hook

*The size of the wearer will determine how much fleece and ribbon you'll need to buy. To measure for different-sized ponchos, have the intended wearer hold both arms out horizontally from her body. Measure from fingertip to fingertip to calculate the size of the fabric square you'll need. Our extra-roomy poncho used 1½ yards of fleece.

**We used two large economy-sized bags of beads made by Darice.

Poncho pattern

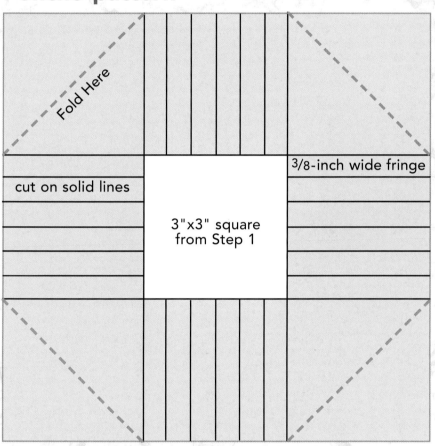

Fold Here

cut on solid lines

3/8-inch wide fringe

3"x3" square
from Step 1

Top of poncho with fringe and fold lines indicated. (See Steps 1 and 2.)

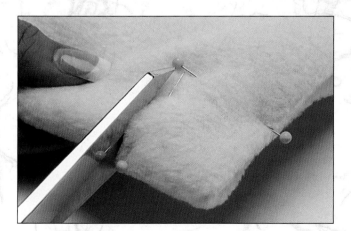

1 Cut selvage edges off of fleece. Cut remaining two edges evenly to create a perfect square.

Fold fabric into quarters, making sure edges are lined up evenly. In the center folded corner, mark a 1½-inch square. Leaving the fleece folded, cut out the square. When poncho is unfolded, you should have a 3-inch square in the center of the poncho.

The diagram above shows the cut center section, and the fold and cut lines you will follow in Step 2.

2 Leaving an uncut square in each corner of the neck section, mark and cut six $3/8$-inch wide by 3-inch long fringe pieces as shown in the diagram on page 81.

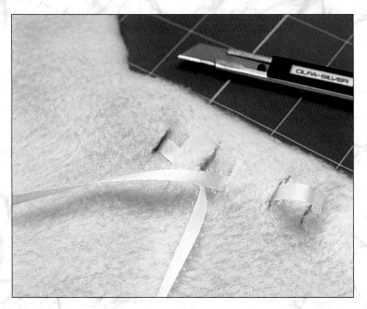

3 With each corner on neck, fold point toward inside and pin in place. Cut $3/8$-inch wide by $5/16$-inch long slits about $1/2$ inch apart as shown.

Using a 24-inch piece of ribbon, weave ribbon through slits by starting in the front, weaving to the back, and continuing back to front. Tie in a bow to finish each section.

4 Using a steel crochet hook, push two fringe ends through bead (it's easier to push one piece through at a time). Repeat on all four sides.

At left is the neck section as it should look after Step 4.

5 Cut out 3-inch squares from each corner on the outer edges of your poncho.

To create fringe pieces along the sides of the poncho, we found it easiest to cut 12 fringe pieces at a time and then proceed with Step 6 on that section. Repeat with 12 more fringe cuts. This way, you will be sure to end up with even numbers of fringe pieces for your beading.

Begin to cut ³/8-inch wide by 3-inch long fringe pieces.

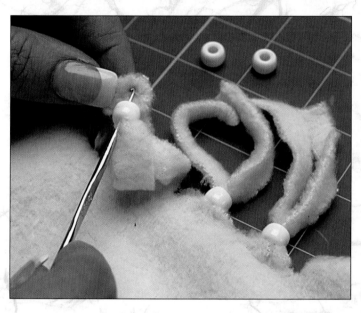

6 Using the steel crochet hook, push two fringe ends through a bead, one piece at a time.

7 Then take side-by-side fringe pieces and attach another bead. Keep staggering your beads to give a lacy effect.

Press and trim any curled fringe pieces, if needed.

5 minutes
for *Shadowboxes*

Turn any small memento into a piece of art.

Small mementos often carry big memories. You might have saved your grandmother's skate key or a handful of marbles from an older brother. Whatever the item, these little treasures shouldn't be tucked away in drawers or hidden in boxes in the attic.

That's where these special shadowboxes work so well.

These two samples may inspire you to create your own special boxful of memories to display, or to pass on to a friend or family member as a terrific, inexpensive gift.

"Billy" Shadowbox

Are you loaded with old family photos but looking for a different way to display them? One terrific way to make a shadowbox is to scan a favorite picture and print it out in black and white. Use watercolor pencils to highlight selected sections of your photo, which will give it a wonderful, old-world feel.

You can add additional images in a creative way by mounting them inside unique frames, such as the image we used here inside the large, round tag.

Use the space in the box to add any item that has meaning to you (or for the intended recipient of this great gift). Add an antique bottle, a bike horn, or a fancy old hairbrush and hang your round tag from that. You can stain wooden letter tags to make them look old, and then spell out a name or sentiment as part of the presentation.

This box had brass corners, and to make them look old, we wiped them with a greenish blue acrylic paint and then wiped them again with white paint to give the metal a faux patina of age.

"Mom" Shadowbox

This garden-inspired shadowbox was designed as a tribute to Mom. In this example, the small, sliding door wooden box came unpainted from a local craft store. Once you've selected a "frame" for your box, let your imagination run wild as you decorate it. You can paint it, stain it, use crayons to color it, or even wrap it in an old newspaper or section of comics.

To decorate this particular box, the wood was sprayed with two coats of a light-colored spray paint, then sandpaper was used to rough up certain sections so that the wood beneath showed through. The entire box was then rubbed with wood stain, which gave the piece an even more authentic aged look.

This one was further embellished by lining it with a coordinating decorative paper applied with spray adhesive. Images were cut from additional paper and decoupaged on the doors and the inside back of the box. (You could also use fabric, or any other material that has a special meaning to you.)

To add images, photocopy or scan a picture and mount on card stock with spray adhesive. Add a 1-inch folded tab on the bottom of the card stock to make the picture stand up. You can use a computer to print out dates, address, descriptions, or any other information you wish, to help your box tell a story.

An Easy Centerpiece

Invite the gang over for a party on the Fourth, and use these adorable painted pots to create individual place settings.

This project provides a fun two-for-one. First, you can use the finished piece, with all the small pots nestled inside the large saucer, as a decorative centerpiece. When the burgers come off the grill, simply place a small pot, complete with utensils and a napkin, at each seat, and your guests will feel both special and appreciated!

You Will Need

- Six 2½-inch clay pots
- One 4-inch clay pot
- One 3-inch clay saucer
- One 10-inch clay saucer
- Clear acrylic sealer with a satin finish
- White acrylic paint (we used Plaid FolkArt, No. 649 Warm White)
- Light blue acrylic paint (we used Plaid FolkArt, No. 402 Light Blue)
- ¾-inch flat brush
- Thick craft glue
- Craft stick
- Ruler
- Scissors
- 1-inch ribbon of your choice
- 36 white buttons
- Bunch of silk flowers
- Pencil
- Self-adhesive felt, light blue

Getting Started

Spray the inside and outside of all clay saucers and pots with one coat of clear acrylic sealer. Let dry completely.

Using acrylic paint, paint the insides of all the pots and saucers white. Paint the outsides of all clay saucers and pots light blue. Let dry.

Spray again with two coats of sealer, letting dry between coats.

1 Turn the large pot upside down. Apply glue to the bottom of the small saucer along the raised ridge and place it on the bottom of the pot, gently pressing the two pieces together to ensure good adhesion (photo 1a). Let dry. Measure and cut a 10-inch length of ribbon. Wrap the ribbon around the bottom of the large pot so the ribbon covers the area where the saucer and pot meet. Turn the end of the ribbon under, overlap in back, and secure with glue (photo 1b). Let dry.

2 Measure and cut six additional 10-inch lengths of ribbon. Apply glue to the back side of the ribbons and wrap around the rims of the small pots, turning the ends under and overlapping in back. Secure ends down with glue. Let dry. Apply glue to the back sides of six buttons and space them evenly around the rims over the ribbons. Let dry.

3 Cut the stems from the flowers as close to the petals as possible. (NOTE: If petals separate, glue the layers together.) Apply glue to the back sides of the flowers and secure around the rim of the large pot. Let dry.

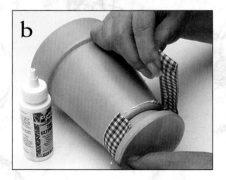

4 Trace around the bottoms of the small pots on the paper side of the felt. Cut out and remove the paper backing and adhere to bottoms of the pots. Cut out four additional ½-inch circles and adhere to the bottom of the large saucer.

5 minutes for Valentine's Day

Remember Valentine's Day! Take a moment to do something special for a friend or sweetheart.

Sweet Shoes and Socks

Slippers or shoes can be dressed up for a special evening with heart appliqués, ribbon, lace, or glitter. Try your hand at dolling up a sweetie's socks or shoes for a sparkling surprise. You can iron on appliqués or stretch-stitch the lace and ribbon on socks or slippers. Tack a bow at the back of a pair of socks, or consider adding a velvet bow to your shoes for a final touch.

Sparkling Wine

Have a little leftover red holiday sugar from the last batch of Christmas cookies? Consider this sweet way to tell someone special how much you care.

You'll need two champagne flutes or wine glasses, a square of double-sided sticky tape with peel-off backing, and a bit of corn syrup.

For the heart on the glass, simply cut your double-sided tape into a heart shape and place on the glass. Sprinkle colored sugar on the design, and press gently to secure. (Most of these sticky tapes release when they are wet, so your design will disappear when you wash the glass.)

For the edge of the glass, dip the rim into a bit of corn syrup and then into the sugar.

Tie a bow on the stem, and drink to your future!

The Door to Love

This cute little item looks terrific hanging from a bedroom doorknob. Simply sew and stuff five little hearts in a variety of fabrics, add a thick ribbon to each for hanging, and then gather this handful of hearts together at the top of the ribbon in a bow.

You can further adorn the hearts with small "flowers" made of circles of the same fabric, stitched through the center of the heart to create a dimple.

Sweet Dreams

Lavender sachets provide soothing scents, and this colorful pillow doubles as a drawer freshener or an attractive dresser decoration.

Simply cut two sheets of fabric into a heart shape, stitch, and turn inside out. Stuff the pillow with a mix of fiberfill and a generous handful of dried lavender.

You can embellish this with tiny rosettes by piercing through the pillow with a large needle, stringing the rosette on the front, and then pulling to create a pucker. (This sweet pillow might even be worth a kiss!)

Sweet Tooth

Have a chocoholic friend who could use a little lift? Dip a spoon into a melted mixture of chocolate chips and then let the chocolate harden. (You can sprinkle the still-melted chocolate with matching ingredients, such as crushed peppermints, before it hardens, for a little something extra special.) Wrap the spoon in cellophane, attach a ribbon, and put it in a special coffee cup along with a handful of individual cocoas. You'll make someone's day a little brighter!

A Handwoven Bag

Create a tiny tote out of leftover yarn. This super-simple project shows you how!

Weaving is one of the oldest art forms, and with this clever little project, you'll learn the basics of the technique at its simplest. These neat little bags are perfect for carrying a few essentials to the beach, or just to the corner store.

For a variation on this bag, try following the steps below using ¼-inch strips of fabric for a "rag rug" effect.

You Will Need

- Heavy cardboard or book board (sized for your bag)
- Yarn (we used Caron 4-ply Rainbow Dreams yarn)
- Metal yarn needle
- Thread (in a color to coordinate with the yarn)
- Tapestry needle
- Crochet cotton or embroidery floss
Optional:
- Beads

SPECIAL PROJECT TIP

In weaving, threads are not knotted together when you reach the end of your yarn or string. When you run out of yarn, leave a 2-inch tail and add the new ball by starting four stitches back in the same pattern as the last four stitches of the previous ball.

Simply lay in your next piece of yarn, tucking in ends, and continue weaving.

1 Cut a piece of cardboard the size you want your tote to be. (Ours was roughly 4 by 8 inches.) Wrap a warp thread (yarn) around the cardboard from the front to the back the long way and tie it together. Continue wrapping the warp threads until you have 19 to 25 threads on each side. (There must be an uneven number on each side.) Tie the last two threads together on the opposite short side.

Roll several small balls of yarn into easy-to-handle small sizes. Thread the end of one ball of yarn onto the yarn needle. (This yarn is known as the weft.) Starting at one edge of the bottom of your cardboard and leaving about a 2-inch tail piece of yarn outside your cardboard loom, use your yarn needle to go under the first thread, over the second, under the third, and so on. Continue, turning the cardboard over to continue the weaving on the other side. (See Special Project Tip for instructions on using additional balls of yarn.)

2 As you weave in each piece of yarn, lay it down in an arc. This way, when you use your needle to push the yarn down tight against the previous layers of weaving, the fit will be snug but not too tight. You can use your needle to push down the yarn on each row or you can use a comb or fork to snug the rows together.

4 Choose the same yarn or a contrasting crochet thread or embroidery floss and begin stitching over the top edge of the bag. Do not cut the threads tied in Step 3—simply hold them down and stitch over them.

Make even stitches all the way around the top of the bag. Leave the last 2-inch tail, cut the yarn, and weave the tail into the top row of stitches.

Thread in any extra tails to the inside of the bag, and cut off excess.

3 Continue weaving until your bag is at least 6 inches high. At 6 inches, leave a 2-inch tail; cut the yarn.

Carefully cut the threads at the top of the cardboard. Tie two threads at a time together, side by side. After all yarns have been tied to a neighboring piece, remove cardboard.

SPECIAL PROJECT TIPS

- After Step 4, you can further embellish the top of your bag by adding beads. Do this by double-threading and knotting a tapestry needle and then running the needle from the inside of the bag to the outside at the bottom of the top row of one of the stitches. Put two or three beads on the thread and stitch into the middle of that top stitch. Continue around the top of the bag, sewing bunches of two or three beads.

- You can add a handle of beads to this bag or braid or weave a handle out of additional yarn. (Use four strands of yarn or cord when braiding a handle.) Sew the handle in place inside the bag at each side.

That's Hot! Jean Jewelry

In just a few minutes, you can add some real sparkle to your jeans.

You can use any grouping of charms, chains, or beading cord to make jean jewelry. In this example, beads were added by attaching a piece of wire to a link on a chain, and then beads were strung on the wire. After the last bead was added, we simply wound the wire tightly between the last two beads and trimmed it as close as possible.

Using charms and initials for a special person can make a great and very personal gift. We found these inexpensive initial charms at an "everything for a dollar" store.

Latch onto a hot trend that's perfect for back to school. You can make these jean trinkets from either broken pieces of vintage jewelry, or you can create all-new items from craft store materials. (This is a particularly nice way to show off earrings that have lost their mates, or make use of old brooches that have lost their pins.)

You Will Need

- At least a 5-inch length of chain
- 2 needle-nosed pliers
- Two 10 mm jump rings*
- One 14 mm lobster claw fastener
- Charms, old or new jewelry pieces, baubles and trinkets, large beads

Optional:
- Various beads
- Beading thread

Jump rings and lobster claws can be found in the jewelry section of your favorite craft or beading store. You may need various sizes of jump rings to add your charms and baubles, but you can purchase economy packs that contain many different-sized items.

1 For the chain jean jewelry: We started with a piece of chain about 5 inches long. We used two needle-nosed pliers to gently separate a link and split our chain into pieces about 1½ inches long, and 3½ inches long. Fold the 3½-inch piece in half and connect the 1½-inch piece in the center, squeezing the removed link back together to attach them. You should now have a chain that looks like a Y.

2 Attach jump rings to the top of each arm of the Y, and then add a lobster claw to one side to create a way to fasten the piece around a belt loop. You can add any charms and baubles you like to the middle and end of the jean jewelry using additional jump rings. TIP: If you want a longer jean gem chain, start with a longer chain length.

This eye-catching piece is an amulet from an old necklace. To remove the amulet, we spread the links on the old necklace, and removed as much of the chain as we needed to shorten the piece. We reconnected the chain, leaving the original clasp in place. We then added four small chains with beads to the bottom.

Simple beading projects make great jean jewelry. You can let your imagination go wild and combine any items that catch your fancy.

SPECIAL PROJECT TIPS

- To make blue beaded jean jewel at left, use beading thread and tie a bead at the end of a 12-inch length of double thread. Run both threads up a center set of beads and then split threads to the left and right to form a circle that will go around a belt loop. Double knot the thread onto jump rings, trim and add a lobster claw or other fastener at one side.

- For gold beaded jean jewel use 4 single lengths of thread, knotting a bead at the bottom, then use photo as guide and add fastener at end (same as above).

A Romantic *Bath*

Create a one-of-a-kind mosaic birdbath using easy-to-obtain hardware and craft supplies.

ho says our feathered
friends don't have an eye
for beauty?
We decided to add a little art to a
plain concrete birdbath by creating a
mosaic in the bowl. This project takes
about a weekend to make, to allow for
drying time, but if you take care to
protect the birdbath during cold
weather, this project will provide years
of enjoyment for both you and your
backyard guests.

You Will Need

- Concrete birdbath (two-piece birdbaths
  are easiest to work with so you can remove
  the bowl as you work)
- Brown paper, scissors, and pencil
- Variety of home improvement tiles, mosaic
  craft tiles, glass beads, and so on (the
  amount required will depend on the size
  of your birdbath)
- Bucket, water, and sponge
- Tile cutters and safety glasses
- Master Blend Standard Thin-Set Mortar*
- Acrylic Mortar Mix*
- Small notched trowel*

- Medium-sized palette knife*
- Several dozen ⅛- to ½-inch grout joints*
- PolyBlend Sanded Grout*
- TileLab Surface Guard Penetrating Sealer*

*These products are specially designed to work
in areas where water is present. We purchased
all of these items at our local Home Depot
home improvement store. (The materials
listed are also used for swimming pool applications.) It's important to purchase a good quality
sealer to protect your birdbath in order to
ensure that your project lasts for years.

1 Create a paper template following the shape
of the inside of the bowl of the birdbath. (To
do this, cut a large circle of brown paper the
same size as your bowl. You may need to cut a
hole in the center of the paper template to help
it lie flat inside your curved bowl.)

Use a marker to create a starting point on
both the birdbath and the template. Remove the
paper template and place on a flat surface.
NOTE: When working on this project it is best
to be in an area that will be undisturbed.

In order to get your pattern started, arrange
a variety of tiles on the surface of the birdbath.
Once you are happy with your pattern,

transfer your tile placement to the
paper template. Continue placing
tiles on your paper template until
you have your desired look. You
can create smaller, irregular pieces
of tile by using a tile cutter to snip

sections off of larger tiles, such as
those intended for use in a kitchen
or bath. (Wear safety glasses
whenever cutting larger tiles into
smaller pieces.)

a

2 PLACING TILES: Mix the Master-Blend Thin-Set mortar with the Acrylic Mortar Mix according to manufacturer's directions. Spread mixture in a small area in the center of the bowl with notched trowel or palette knife. TIP: Work in one small area at a time to keep the mortar from drying out.

Transfer your tiles from the paper template to the birdbath according to your pattern. Use grout joints or tile spacers to keep the distance between pieces of tile uniform. These small spacers are inserted at the edge of the tiles, and the next tile is then placed to abut the spacer (photo 2a).

NOTE: We found that the easiest way to work with our tile placement was to start with the center. We then set tiles around the upper rim of our birdbath. This let us adapt the tile placement in between these two sets of tile as we needed to accommodate small irregularities due to the shape of the bowl (photo 2b).

b

SPECIAL PROJECT TIP

If you have a spare Lazy Susan, place the bowl of the birdbath on the turntable. That way, the bowl can be rotated as you apply your tiles, which saves you a lot of work.

3 Continue to transfer the tiles from your template to the birdbath. Using tile cutters, cut mosaic tiles into smaller pieces to fill in any gaps in your design. Alternate the colors and shapes, leaving 1/8-inch gaps for grout joints. TIP: Working with small pieces of tile can be difficult. Apply the Thin-Set Mortar Mix to the back of the tiles rather than to the birdbath to ensure that the tiles adhere firmly in place.

a

4 After all the tiles are in place, allow the Thin-Set to dry for at least 24 hours before grouting. Mix grout according to manufacturer's instructions. Trowel a large dollop of grout onto the surface of the birdbath and spread it out with a margin trowel (photo 4a). Make sure that there is a good, even covering and that all the joints have been filled. Immediately wipe the surface with a damp sponge to remove excess grout. Wipe grout away until the surface is completely clean (photo 4b). Let dry for 24 hours.

To finish your birdbath, wipe the surface with a damp, lint-free cloth, and then seal the grout with TileLab Surface Guard Penetrating Sealer, following manufacturer's instructions.

NOTE: Protect your project during winter months by removing any standing water in the bowl and covering the entire birdbath with plastic.

b

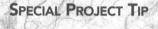

SPECIAL PROJECT TIP

Because any birdbath bowl will have sloping sides, it's easiest to work with pieces of tile that are no larger than 2 inches to make placement easier. We found that using some small tiles mounted on a mesh background was also helpful. (These tiles are generally sold by the square foot at any shop that carries tile for homes.)

A Romantic Bath

A Sparkling
Centerpiece

Make an old basket the star of your table with some updated asymmetrical beading.

Adding a little flash to inexpensive items around the house is a quick way to put a personal stamp on your decor. For this easy project, we turned an inexpensive basket into an eye-catching centerpiece with an easy beading technique. (This would make a fantastic decorative center point for your Thanksgiving feast!)

You Will Need*

- Basket (we used an Appalachian-style basket 11 inches tall and 8 inches across)
- One roll 26-gauge gold wire
- One 1¼-ounce package of Antique Gold Bead Ancient Treasures
- One box crystal and amber Classic Glass Beads No. 87968
- Round-nosed pliers
- Towel

*We found all of our supplies for this project at our local Michael's craft store. The basket is a Vintage Collection basket from Decor International. Antique gold beads are manufactured by Westrim Crafts and the crystal and amber beads are manufactured by Bead Heaven. Wild Wire makes the wire and the round-nosed pliers we used.

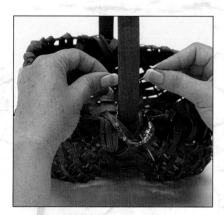

1 Place a towel over your work area so dropped beads will not roll onto the floor. Cut a piece of gold wire about 36 inches long. Place enough beads on one end of the wire to completely encircle the basket handle. Start by putting three of the smallest beads in the box on the wire. Follow with one large glass bead, three small beads, and one large gold bead, and so on. Wrap the beads around the basket handle. Pull wire taut and wrap short end around the longer piece of wire to secure. The beads will now cover the handle without wire showing.

SPECIAL PROJECT TIPS

- We liked the look of an asymmetrical beaded rim on our basket, but if you purchase additional beads, you can easily continue this technique around the entire rim of your basket.

- Once you've completed this project, you can use the basket year-round as a table centerpiece by filling it with different seasonal items. Consider Halloween treats for a spooky party, autumn leaves or pheasant feathers for an autumn flavor, or even mixed and matched Christmas ornaments for a holiday feel.

2 Starting from the inside of the basket, string enough beads on the wire to reach the first place that you can push the wire between the weaving and the rim, from the front to the inside. Use three small beads, one large glass bead, three small beads, one gold bead, and three small beads. The wire should be pulled tight as it wraps over the rim with no bare wire showing.

Repeat this process across the rim to the middle of one side. Add wire as needed by attaching new wire to old wire between beads on the inside of the basket. Wrap new wire over and over to attach. Continue beading back along the rim toward the handle. We now have added two rows of beads on the rim. When you have reached the handle, add five to six rows up the handle.

3 Add a new piece of wire at the end of one of the rim bead strands. This last row across the rim will be done with the smaller glass beads and the smallest glass beads and will fill in any holes that exist. Work this row by going through the beads that are in place.

Thread on the beads needed to fill in the space and go through a bead in one of the strands. Continue across the row. Fasten wire at the end of the row.

4 To make the dangling beads, cut a piece of wire 6 inches long. With the round-nosed pliers, hold one cut end and wrap wire three times around the pliers. String beads on half of the wire. Thread the other end around a wire between beads and twist to hold in place. String beads on the end and trim excess wire allowing ¾ inch. Twist wire around pliers to finish. Add five to six dangling bead pairs.

Designer
Decorating

Punch up the style in your home with these classy projects! Paint a gorgeous welcome mat. Design an elegant collage. Create a classic curtain. These projects will help you add designer details both inside and out. The reward comes in all the compliments you get ... and then basking in the glory of a stylish home.

Accessible *Art*

Use outdoor canvas fabric as the base for a beautiful painted floor cloth that is surprisingly durable.

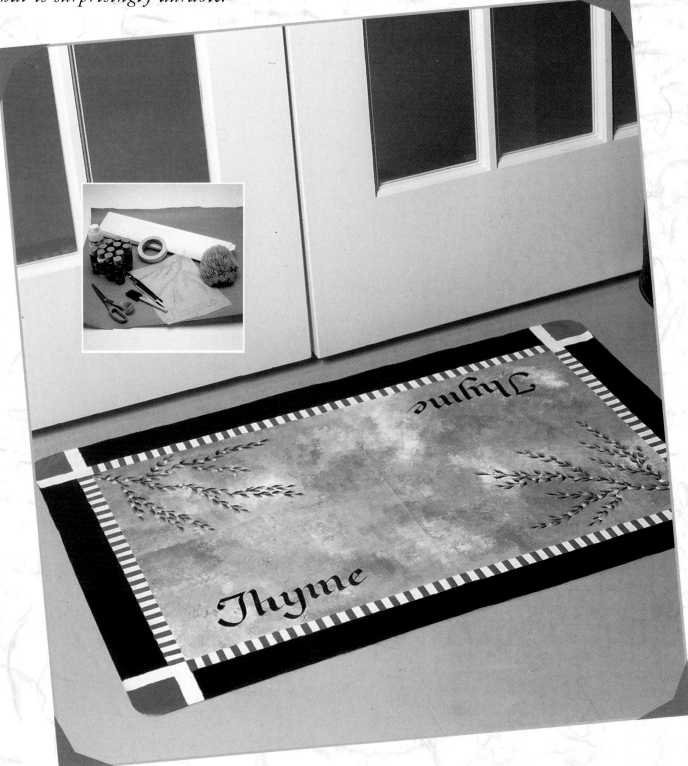

Looking for a durable floor cloth that has a bit of personality? Consider painting your own, using inexpensive outdoor canvas fabric as your, well, canvas!

This fabric takes paint well, and holds up nicely once you've sealed your design.

This is a particularly fun project for use on a deck or patio to add a bit of color to your outside area. Be aware, however, that using this project outdoors may fade your colors and shorten the floor cloth's usable life.

You Will Need

- ⅔ yard white outdoor canvas fabric*
- Scissors
- ¾-inch masking tape
- Disposable plate
- Paper towels
- Water basin
- Acrylic craft paint**
- Sponge
- 1-inch sponge-tipped brush
- Artist's brushes***

- Pencil
- Graphite paper (black)
- Tracing paper
- Interior/exterior non-yellowing sealer**

*Rockland Industries makes a product called Roc-lon Multi Purpose Cloth that will not fray when cut, which makes it perfect for this use. The heavyweight material accepts paint well, and is available at most local sewing stores.

**We used DecoArt Americana paint in Antique Maroon, Baby Pink, Dark Chocolate, Fawn, Hauser Dark Green, Jade Green, Lamp Black, Light Buttermilk, Mississippi Mud, Traditional Raw Sienna, Warm White, and Williamsburg Blue, as well as DecoArt Multi-Purpose Sealer.
***We used Loew-Cornell Golden Taklon brushes and fabric brush.

1 Cut canvas fabric 21½ by 32 inches. Round the corners to prevent them from rolling up.

Place a line of masking tape 2 inches away from the edge of each canvas fabric edge to mask off border. Paint outer corners Williamsburg Blue and outer border Antique Maroon with acrylic paint. Let dry.

2 Using the sponge, dip into Light Buttermilk, Fawn, and Mississippi Mud. Pounce center area of floor cloth and blend to achieve a faux finish. Remove masking tape and let dry.

3 Using a No. 10 brush, paint Williamsburg Blue stripes along masked border, omitting the corner areas. Let dry.

4 Freehand the thyme sprigs or use the pattern below. If you are using the pattern, trace it using a pencil and tracing paper. Slip graphite paper between tracing paper and floor cloth. Retrace pattern onto the floor cloth. Using liner brush, dip into Traditional Raw Sienna and Dark Chocolate to paint stems.

Floor Cloth Pattern

Enlarge at 285%

5 Using the No. 10 flat shader, dip into Jade Green on one side of the brush and Hauser Dark Green on the other side of the brush. Paint leaves on each stem.

6 Dip fabric brush into Baby Pink and Warm White. Touch onto stems for thyme blossoms.

7 Using the No. 10 flat shader, paint Lamp Black lettering for 'Thyme'.

8 Using the sponge-tipped brush, apply several coats of a non-yellowing sealer onto the dry floor cloth, letting each coat dry completely before applying the next coat.

SPECIAL PROJECT TIP

You may want to consider using a piece of rug liner to anchor the floor cloth. Cut the rug liner slightly smaller than your floor cloth, and then place the liner underneath the painted cloth. You can attach the liner to the back of your floor cloth with any good quality adhesive that will work on fabric.

Classic *Curtain*

Want to create a more private space to conceal an area in your home?
Consider a curtain!

One of the unique challenges in this basement room is that the space is actually used in two different ways: as a lounging area, and as office space for the homeowner. An alcove tucked behind a built-in bookshelf contains a desk area and a drafting table, both of which are often in use. The need, then, was to find a way to visually close off this space while still making it part of the overall room. Since whatever option we chose would be a large visual element in the room, we decided that we needed to make this divider as elegant and attractive as possible.

To do that, we first decided that we needed to create a curtain to divide the space. A sliding curtain takes up much less space than a door while still letting the occupant of the office feel connected to the larger space. In addition, since this basement room does not offer as much natural light as do rooms with more windows, we wanted the fabrics we selected to be welcoming and dramatic to help improve the "coziness" factor of the space.

We decided to splurge and use silks to create this curtain but fabrics such as satin or even polyester would work equally well and give the curtains a nice silky appearance. You can follow the techniques here using less expensive fabrics to get an equally attractive room divider, or you can use more costly fabric and let this curtain be a signature item in your room. The choice is yours.

NOTE: In French, this type of curtain is known as a *portière*, in essence, a "door" made of fabric.

Getting Started

This curtain is designed to hang from a suspended curtain rod with attachable clips, available in any sewing or home improvement store. Our rod was 48 inches wide, not including the decorative finials. The length from the bottom of our rings to the floor was 75 inches.

That gave us the finished width and length of our curtain—50 inches wide (we rounded up), and 75 inches long.

We knew that we wanted to add decorative bouillion fringe to the bottom of our curtain. (Particularly with silky fabrics, the added weight of the trim helps a curtain to hang more smoothly.)

We cut our fabric like this: Since the trim we selected was 5 inches long, we decided to make our bottom edge a double, 5-inch hem. (That requires 10 inches of additional length for each drapery panel. A deep hem also helps to stabilize lightweight fabrics.)

Add 1 inch for seam allowances, and our cut length became 86 inches.

We determined the cut width of our fabrics like this: The general rule when cutting fabric for a box-pleated curtain is to cut the material two times desired fullness, plus your seam allowances.

For our front panel, we cut four strips of one fabric 18 inches wide and 86 inches long, and cut two strips of coordinating fabric 18 inches wide and 86 inches long. (That's enough to make each of the two finished panels 25 inches wide.)

For our back panel, we cut 2 widths of our solid colored silk 54 inches wide and 86 inches long.

You Will Need

- 5 yards, 54-inch-wide silk toile fabric
- 7½ yards, 54-inch-wide silk solid fabric
- 3 yards, 5-inch bouillion fringe
- 3 yards, 4-inch buckram or fusible buckram
- Thread
- Scissors
- Pins
- Iron
- Covered buttons—16 ⅞-inch buttons for the front and 8 1¼-inch buttons for the back
Optional
- Fusible hem

SPECIAL PROJECT TIP

When combining fabrics, it is important to use ones that have the same fiber content. This will alleviate any problems when cleaning the drapery as well as ensuring that they will hang properly when sewn together.

1 Sew your three strips of fabric together for each front panel using ½-inch seam allowance, alternating fabrics: pattern–plain–pattern. Repeat for the other panel.
  Press seams open.

2 Make a 5-inch, double-hem at the bottom of each front and back panel. To make the hem, measure up from the bottom edge 5 inches, turn, and press. Turn the hem allowance again, press, and pin in place.
  Sew hem in place keeping stitches as close to rolled edge as possible. TIP: If you would like to conceal your stitching, you can use a blind stitch or fusible hem. Repeat on remaining panels.

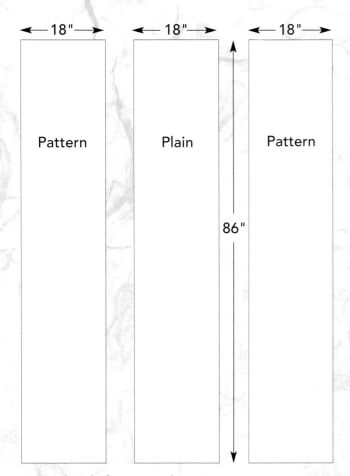

← 18" →	← 18" →	← 18" →
Pattern	Plain	Pattern

86"

Our cut lengths for one panel.

3 Pin trim 5 inches up from the bottom edge on the right side of each front panel. Sew in place.

4 Place back panel on work surface right side up. With right sides together, place front panel over the back panel. Line up the raw edges at the top as well as one of the selvaged edges. Pin in place.

Trim fabric from opposite selvaged edge, making the front panel the same size as the back panel, and pin. Sew around the sides and top edge using ½-inch seam allowance.

5 Measure the width of the panel. Cut buckram 1 inch shorter than this measurement.

If you are using fusible buckram, pin in place, lining up the top edge of the buckram with stitching line. Press, removing pins as you go.

If you are using non-fusible buckram, pin in place, lining up the top edge of the buckram with the raw edge of the fabric. Sew in place using ¼-inch seam allowance.

Turn panels right side out and press.

6 Our finished flat panel measured 51 inches wide.

In order to fit our rod, our panel needs to be 25 inches after pleating, therefore we need to pleat in 26 inches. To do that, we used 8 inches of fabric for the two center pleats and 5 inches on each end pleat, creating a half pleat. The seam where the two fabrics meet will become the center of each pleat.

Lay your panel on your work surface with the top edge of the panel toward you. Measure 4 inches out from each side of the seam and pin mark. Repeat, measuring 2 inches out from seam.

7 Fold the fabric at the 4-inch pin mark and bring it toward seam at the center, folding the fabric again at the 2-inch pin mark. Pin in place. Repeat with remaining center pleat.

8 Measure 5 inches in from the outside edge of the panel and pin mark. Repeat measuring 2½ inches in from edge of panel. Fold the fabric at the 5-inch pin mark and bring it toward the outside edge of the panel, folding the fabric again at the 2½ inch pin mark.
   Pin in place and repeat at opposite side.
   Repeat steps 6 thru 8 with remaining panel.

9 Tack box pleats in place at the bottom edge of the buckram. Keep stitching within ⅝ inch in order to conceal stitching behind the buttons.

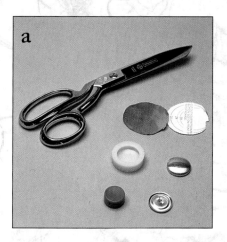

a

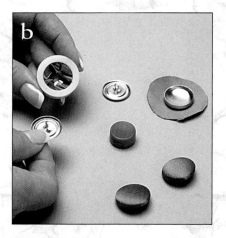

b

10 Cover buttons. The manufacturer's directions are very clear on the packaging: Cut the fabric to the appropriate size for your buttons—the pattern is on the reverse of the package (photo 10a). Then place the right side of the fabric over the plastic holder and place the button shell in the center of the holder. Tuck the fabric in and place the back over the button. Place the cap over the back and push, snapping the back of the button in place (photo 10b).

a

11 Sew buttons in place centering them over the pleat. Here the first button covered our stitching line at the base of the pleat. The second one was placed about ½ inch lower (photo 11a). We then added buttons on the opposite side of our curtain to add detail, as well as cover our stitching (photo 11b).

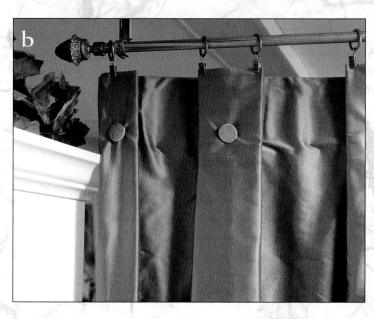

b

A Copper *Trellis*

A trip to your local hardware store will provide the supplies to make this sparkling trellis for less than $75.

Outdoor decorating—whether in the garden or on the patio—has become a much-loved summer activity. Unique decorative details add visual interest to any outside area.

We decided to create a cute copper trellis on a budget to add some detail to the front of this home. All of our supplies came from a local home improvement store, and the price of this trellis is hundreds of dollars less than similar items we found at area garden stores.

The skills involved in this trellis couldn't be easier. You'll also find that you can complete the entire piece in a weekend or less.

You Will Need

- Work gloves
- Four 8-foot sections of ¾-inch copper pipe*
- Measuring tape
- Pencil
- Pipe cutter**
- 18 ¾-inch 'T' joints (used to connect sections of pipe)
- Rubber mallet
- Paper, pencil, and ruler to create pattern
- 50 feet of ¼-inch flexible copper tubing (used for refrigerators)
- Metal snips
- Drill and box of No. 8, 1½-inch screws
- Scrap piece of ¾-inch plywood
- Needle-nosed pliers
- Two spools of thin copper wire
- Painter's tape

Optional:
- Epoxy or similar heavy-duty glue appropriate for use on copper

*All the copper items used in this project are readily available in the plumbing section of your local hardware or home improvement store.

**We found that a copper tubing cutter called AutoCut by General Wire Spring Co., worked particularly well for this project, but you can use any similar copper cutting tool. We found the AutoCut at our local Home Depot store.

Special Safety Note:

The edges on copper pipe can be sharp. We recommend wearing gloves when working with this material.

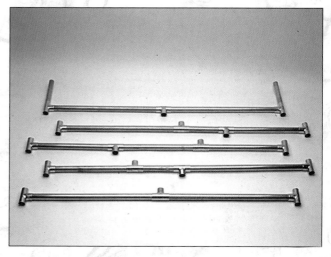

1 Cut the following pieces of copper pipe:

Twelve 18-inch pieces
Seven 12-inch pieces
Six 15-inch pieces
Four 6-inch pieces

NOTE: To cut copper pipe, the pipe cutter is placed over the section to be cut and then rotated to make a clean cut. Some pipe cutters need to be tightened as you rotate them; follow the instructions on the particular pipe cutter you're using.

2 This step is easier if you have a helper.

Following the pattern on page 114, begin to join horizontal pieces of the trellis. The sections will look like the photo above once you've finished.

(We found that the 'T' joints we used fit snugly together; in fact, it helps to use a rubber mallet to hammer the pipe into the 'T' joints to ensure that they are firmly seated.) Because the joints and the pipe fit snugly, we did not solder or glue these sections together. (The wire in Step 6 also serves to hold your trellis together in one piece.)

However, if you like, after you've completed your trellis, you may paint the sections where the pipe and joints meet with a good quality metal glue.

Copper Trellis Pattern

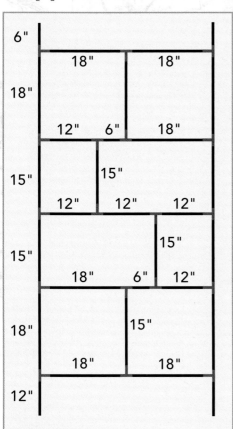

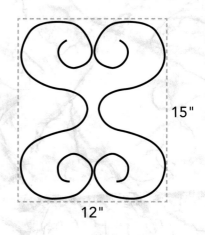

15"

12"

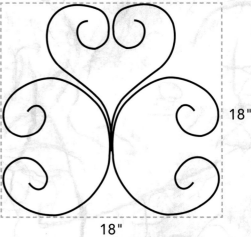

18"

18"

Please Note
The pattern at left shows the sizes and placement for the cut copper pipes you will create in Step 1. The patterns at right show the design we used to create our scrolls in Steps 4 and 5. You can re-create the scroll patterns freehand on appropriately sized paper or, if you wish, you can go to the web site at www.creative-homeartsclub.com, and download full-sized patterns.

3 Join vertical pieces of trellis according to pattern. Once you've finished, your trellis should look like the photo above.

(With the design we used, you'll find that some center sections of the trellis are a fraction of an inch longer than others. This won't matter as you assemble the trellis since the copper is flexible enough to accommodate that variation. You will need to make sure that all of your pipes are inserted into the joints fully, however. Use your rubber mallet to ensure that all pipes are seated firmly.)

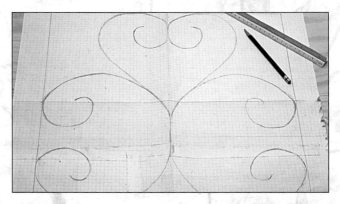

4 To add interest to our trellis, we created a freeform pattern of scrolls that we added to certain inside sections.

The patterns above create designs that fit the top left and bottom right 18-inch sections of the trellis, as well as the 12-inch sections in the middle right and left.

Using the pattern for the 18-inch sections, tape the full-size design to a scrap piece of ¾-inch plywood. (You can download our pattern at www.creativehomeartsclub.com or create your own pattern freehand.)

Drill 1½-inch screws in a double line ¼ inch from each side of your pattern lines. (See the photo in Step 5, opposite. This creates a channel along the pattern that will bend your ¼-inch flexible copper tubing.)

Use a piece of string or a cloth measuring tape to measure the length of flexible tubing needed for your pattern by placing it inside the channel and following the design.

Cut four pieces of ¼-inch flexible tubing equal to this measurement.

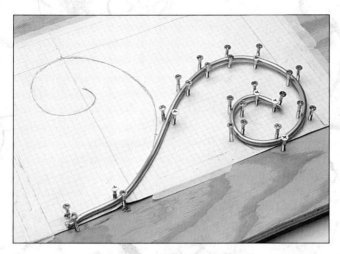

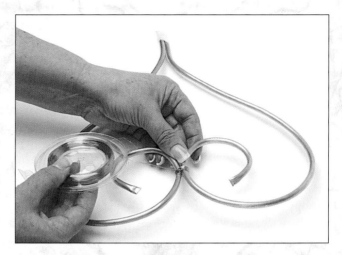

5 Starting at the inside center of your pattern, insert the tubing between the screws, bending the tube and pushing it between the screws as you go. Once the design is complete, carefully remove the tubing. If needed, press the tubing design to make the piece lie flat. TIP: We found it easiest to flatten our piece by stepping on it lightly on a solid surface. (Be sure to protect your flooring with a piece of scrap wood before doing this.)

Repeat this process to complete the rest of the designs for the 18-inch sections, and the designs for the 12-inch sections.

6 Attach the heart-shaped part of the accent pieces together by wrapping a section of them with thin copper wire. Securely wrap the wire around the inside edge of the top of the heart as shown here. Repeat at the bottom of the heart. Attach the side pieces at the base of the heart using this same process.

SPECIAL PROJECT TIP

A heavy book can stand in as a second pair of hands while assembling the scroll accents for this trellis. Place the edge being wrapped beyond the edge of a table. Hold the tubing in place with a heavy book, freeing both hands to wrap the tubing.

a

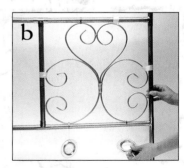

b

7 Place the assembled accent piece (photo 7a) inside the 18-inch section and use tape to hold it in place. Wrap copper wire where the ¼-inch tubing meets the ¾-inch pipe to secure in place (photo 7b). TIP: The flexible copper tubing is very forgiving. You may need to adjust the tubing to make the accent piece sit properly within the square. Repeat with accent pieces for the 12-inch squares.

SPECIAL PROJECT TIP

If you like, you may want to add additional accents to the open sections of your trellis. You can continue the pattern designs in these areas, or you might want to consider adding strings of large, colorful beads strung on thick copper wire.

An Autumn *Collage*

The season inspires this beautiful piece of art.

With autumn breezes beginning to blow, and trees changing colors right before our eyes, consider using leaves in your seasonal decor. Done right, a framed collage can be left up all year long!

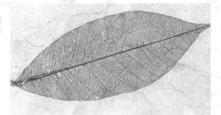

You Will Need

- Decorative papers and card stock (consider texture and pattern when selecting)
- One 8-by-10-inch clip photo frame
- 3 manila shipping tags
- Fine mist spray bottle with water
- Paper Plus Tea Dye Varnish*
- Paintbrush
- 3 "real" leaves or skeleton leaves from your local craft store
- Paper towels
- Bleach and disposable plastic tray
- Pigment inks in coordinating colors
- Rubber stamps**
- Ribbon for tags
- Dry adhesive
- Circular paper clip or other design element

- Xyron 900 Creative Station adhesive system***
- Xyron 150 Create-a-Sticker***
- Metallic leafing pen (optional)

*This product is manufactured by Delta, and you can find it in your local craft or scrap-booking store.

**Our stamps were Time to Enjoy and Harlequin Pattern Block from Hero Arts, stipple background stamp by Annette Allen Watkins for Printworks.

***These special adhesive systems work particularly well for a project like this. They are available at your local craft store, or visit www.xyron.com.

1 PLANNING YOUR BACKGROUND: We chose a textured, dark paper as the background for our design, knowing it would give us good contrast for the tags we wanted to use. Select a paper and cut to size to fit the entire back of your clip frame.

Select a coordinating paper for your second layer. Tear this roughly in half so that it will cover a portion of your background sheet. NOTE: Torn edges always complement a paper project. To tear a more pronounced, exposed edge, hold the section of the paper you wish to use in your non-dominant hand. (Our artist is right-handed, so she held the area she wanted in her left hand.) Using your dominant hand, tear the paper toward you. You can draw a very light pencil line on your paper to guide the direction of your tear. Be sure to erase any stray marks when you are finished.

2 CREATING DISTRESSED TAGS: Begin by crumpling each shipping tag. (TIP: With heavier card stock, it is sometimes easier to start by depressing the center of the tag and then crumpling toward the edges. If your tag tears, don't worry; it will add to the aged look you are trying to achieve.)

Lightly mist a crumpled tag with water. (This will help move the varnish around, as well as concentrate it in the wetter wrinkles.) Now, gently stir the Paper Plus varnish. Don't shake the jar or you will get air bubbles. Brush the moistened tag with a light coat of varnish to start; you can always add more if you want a darker look. Repeat with the other two tags, and set them aside to dry.

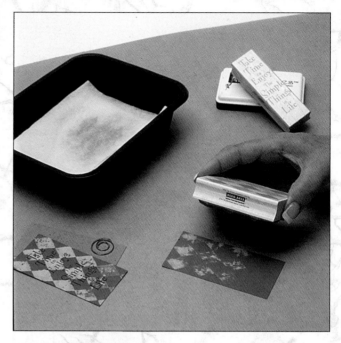

3 SECURING THE SKELETON LEAVES: A product manufactured by the Xyron company called Create-a-Sticker is the ideal adhesive system for delicate, lacy skeleton leaves, or any application where you want quick and complete coverage from an adhesive.* (Glue or tape would show through the openings in each leaf.) This system sandwiches a layer of adhesive between the desired item and a sheet of clear plastic, which you remove to apply.

Drop each leaf into the sticker maker and gently pull on the leading edge of the adhesive. Once the leaf appears on the other side, tear off the sticker. Leaving all the layers together, flip them over and rub the back, making sure you get adhesive on all areas of the leaf. Remove the protective plastic, gently pull the leaf off the paper backing, and place it on one of your dry shipping tags from Step 2. Flip the tag over and gently rub the back to ensure that the leaf is secure. Thread a piece of ribbon through the hole in the tag and set it aside. (See Special Project Tip below.)

4 BLEACHED BACKGROUND: Cut a piece of card stock to fit the text you plan to stamp. Cut a second piece of card stock from a coordinating color to be used to mat your sentiment.

Fold a paper towel in fourths and lay it in the bottom of a disposable plastic tray. Pour a tablespoon or so of bleach onto the paper towel and let it absorb. (Don't use too much bleach or the result will be too bold.) Using the paper towel as an "ink pad," gently tap your background stamp (we used a harlequin pattern) onto the towel. Now stamp directly onto your colored card stock. The bleach will remove some of the pigment from the paper, leaving you with a very artistic, subtle background. Allow this to dry completely before over-stamping it with your sentiment. If the bleached area has not dried, it will cause your inked image to fade. NOTE: Clean your stamp thoroughly to remove any trace of bleach!

SPECIAL PROJECT TIP

When you're adding ribbon to an element such as a scrapbook or in our case, this collage, you'll find that a dry line adhesive runner works well.

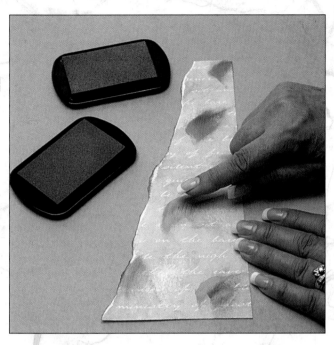

5 DISTRESSING YOUR BACKGROUND PAPER: Using a very light touch, "kiss" the background paper with the corner of your pigment ink pad. Pigment inks remain wet longer than dye inks, allowing you time to smudge the colors with your fingertips as desired. A sanding block can also be used to gently etch the paper's surface. Consider distressing the edges of your paper as well.

Once you've completed distressing your paper and it dries, begin to plan your layout.

In any collage, layout is key. Gather your elements and then play with the arrangement of the pieces you will be using. Don't be afraid to move things around to find the right balance. Sometimes this balance only comes when you eliminate something you originally thought was key to your design. Before you assemble anything, find a look you like.

6 PUTTING IT ALL TOGETHER: We used a second adhesive system made by Xyron to complete our collage (photo 6a).

Using the Xyron 900 with permanent adhesive, run each item through the device, image facing up (photo 6b). It isn't necessary to put adhesive on your largest background sheet. Remove the clips from the frame. Keeping your overall layout in mind, begin placing your background elements first. Secure the sentiment and mat piece with a decorative paper clip. Build your layers up until you have finished. You may find that you need a small amount of adhesive to ensure that the ribbon stays where you want it.

Lay the glass on top of your artwork, and replace the frame clips. Tint the metal clips to match your artwork if you like (copper in our sample), using a metallic marker pen.

Budget *Decorating*

Turn inexpensive ready-made curtains into designer window treatments with these quick tricks.

Interior designers charge clients a lot of money to provide classic decorative touches for a home. One of the more expensive challenges a designer can address is to create window treatments for oddly shaped windows or doors. Custom window treatments for those spaces can easily cost hundreds—if not thousands.

However, with a little creativity, anyone can modify easily available ready-made drapery panels to fit almost any space, and create a designer look without the designer price tag. For this project, we added pinch pleats and tassels to purchased panels for a touch of elegance. You'll find another idea for extra tall windows on page 123.

You'll find another idea for extra tall windows on page 123.

You Will Need

- Three ready-made drapery panels*
- Measuring tape
- Pins
- Scissors
- Drapery hooks
- Wood pole with support brackets, rings, and finials

Optional:
- Decorative tassels

We bought three panels that were 55 inches wide by 84 inches long. Each panel cost about $25. Most ready-made drapery panels measure between 48 and 55 inches wide and are 84 inches long. Some companies now offer ready-mades up to 96 inches long, which gives you further options for working with unique window shapes.

Getting Started

Covering a Sliding Glass Patio Door

Start by measuring your window or door to determine the finished width and finished length you want for your window treatment. One reason custom window treatments look elegant is that the material is very full. (Standard fullness used in custom window treatments is minimum 2.5 times the window opening. That means that if your window opening is 66 inches wide, you multiply 66 x 2.5 = 165 inches of fabric.)

To create this fullness for our sliding door curtain at right, we pinned three panels right sides together and sewed, keeping our stitches just outside the hemmed edge of the ready-made panels. Press seams open. Fold drapery in half to locate the center of the panels and mark with a pin.

SPECIAL PROJECT TIP

If you're working with very light-weight ready-made panels, such as sheers, it's easier to purchase rings with clips—available at any fabric store—to hang your drapery.

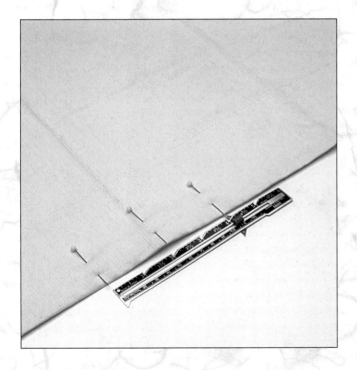

1 Read Getting Started above.

Once we had our three sewn-together panels, we decided to create a more custom look by adding pinch pleats and tassels to the top.

We used 2-prong pleats to accommodate each tassel, and these pleats each use about 4 inches of fabric. If you don't want to add tassels to your curtains, you can create a standard 3-prong pinch pleat, which will use about 6 inches of fabric per pleat.

When working with pinch-pleated headings, the fabric must be carefully divided into pleats and spaces. There are no rules of thumb for calculating the number of pleats and the size of the spaces you leave between pleats. We planned our pleats by measuring 2 inches out from each side of our center marking and then placing a pin to mark our first pleat (giving us the 4 inches of fabric the 2-prong pleat requires). After some calculations, we determined that we could accommodate 12 pinch pleats with rough 9-inch spaces between them to create a soft droop across the top of our window treatment.

Working from the center out, mark each pleat and each space between pleats with a vertical pin. You may need to make adjustments so that the pleats and spaces work out evenly.

2 Fold each pleat wrong sides together, lining up the pins. Hold the pleat in place with a pin. Machine stitch down the line indicated by the pins approximately 3 inches from the top edge of the drapery panel. Repeat with remaining pleats.

3 Lay your drapery down on a large flat surface, right side up. To form the pleat, hold the seam with one hand and fold the pleat in half with your other hand, pushing the center down toward the table so that the sides bulge out (photo 3a). Place a tassel between the folds and pin in place (photo 3b). Machine stitch across the top of each pleat ¼ to ½ inch down from the top edge.

Insert drapery hooks and your drapery is ready to hang.

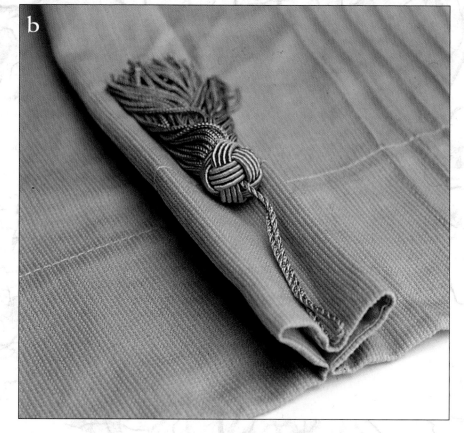

SPECIAL PROJECT TIP

When you buy several ready-made panels, it is not unusual to find that they are slightly different lengths. If you want to sew the panels together, as we did in the project here, sew all panels together, but stop stitching a few inches above the bottom hem. Undo the hems, align your bottom edges, and re-hem so that they are all exactly the same length.

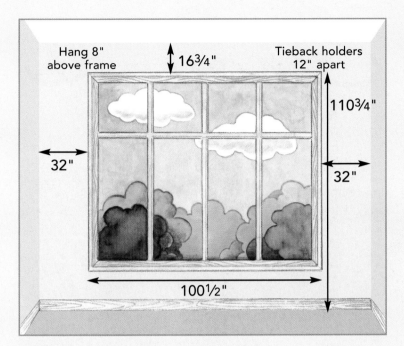

Hang 8" above frame

16¾"

Tieback holders 12" apart

110¾"

32"

32"

100½"

Problem:

Ready-made drapery panels can come to the rescue in a number of different ways for unusually shaped windows.

In this example, the problem is a common one often found in newer construction—a very large window that is both extra tall and extra wide. A professional interior designer could charge as much as $1,500 to dress this window, but you can do it yourself for about $150.

Solution:

The trick with a window like this is to add both length and style to plain, inexpensive drapery panels. The challenge is that ready-made panels will seldom be long enough to reach from the top of this window to the floor. In this case, the window measures 110¾ inches from top of frame to floor, but ready-made panels only come in an 84-inch finished length.

To address this, buy three ready-made drapery panels—two in one color and a third in a coordinating color. To save money on drapery hardware, buy eight inexpensive tieback holders instead of a drapery rod, rings, and finials.

Cut two strips of fabric from the coordinating panel–the length required in this example would be 35 inches plus 1 inch for seam allowances.

Measure from the floor to the bottom edge of the window frame. Mark and measure up from the bottom edge of the remaining two panels equal to this measurement. Cut across the panel at this mark. (The bottom edge of the coordinating panel should sit just below the frame of the window, unifying the vertical lines of the window.)

Attach the coordinating insert using a ½-inch seam allowance. Use the remaining fabric to make small tabs to hang the drapery. (To do this, cut two pieces of fabric 7 inches long and 3 inches wide for each tab. Machine stitch tabs right sides together, leaving one end open. Turn tab right side out. Turn raw edge to the inside of the tab and press. Fold tab in half and pin tabs in place at the top edge of the wrong side of the drapery panel placing one at each end and then equally spacing the remaining tabs between them. Machine stitch along the bottom edge of the tab.)

This casual style of window treatment looks best when the bottom edge of the drapery panel just touches the floor. For a more dramatic look, you could make your panels 6 inches longer than necessary and let the extra material puddle on the floor.

SPECIAL PROJECT TIPS

To hang a window treatment like this, slip the loop of the tab over the post of the tieback holder and then attach the face.

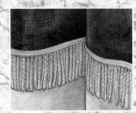

You can sew bullion fringe over the seam to add texture, weight, and a gorgeous custom look to a window treatment.

The Castle Grounds

Learn a simple technique to transform concrete garden objects into faux-aged "classic" statuary.

If you spend any time browsing through decorating books that feature European themes, you'll notice that one of the classic features of these continental gardens is statuary.

These statues, which range from grand in size to small in scope, all share one feature—an aged patina that makes them look as if they have stood on the castle grounds for millennia.

The work of wind, water, and weather all combine to give these statues an age and gravity that new cement statues just can't match.

Unless, of course, you use your talents to fake that aged appearance using common household materials.

We found this new statue of a woman from a local manufacturer who casts a variety of such cement objects.

(You can find similar items at your local home and garden store. Prices vary, but smaller items, such as birdbaths and animals or urns, are generally inexpensive.)

We then mimicked the appearance of an old marble statue with this simple technique.

You Will Need

- Concrete garden item
- Bucket
- Quart-size containers of exterior flat latex paint in dark green and black
- Water
- Rubber gloves
- Small disposable plastic container
- Paintbrushes or disposable sponge brushes (bristle brushes work best)
- Medium-sized artist's brush

Before

1 Mix 2 parts green exterior latex paint (we used about 1 cup) and 1 part black exterior latex paint (we used ½ cup) in a bucket. Add an equal amount of water (1½ cups) and mix thoroughly. The mixture should have a very watery consistency.

Test the paint and water mixture's color consistency by using an artist's brush to paint a bit of it on the back side of your concrete item. Stand back and observe the color. Add more paint to make the final result darker or, if necessary, add water, a tablespoon at a time, to make the mixture lighter and more transparent. The patina on your concrete will fade with exposure to the sun, so it is better to start darker than lighter.

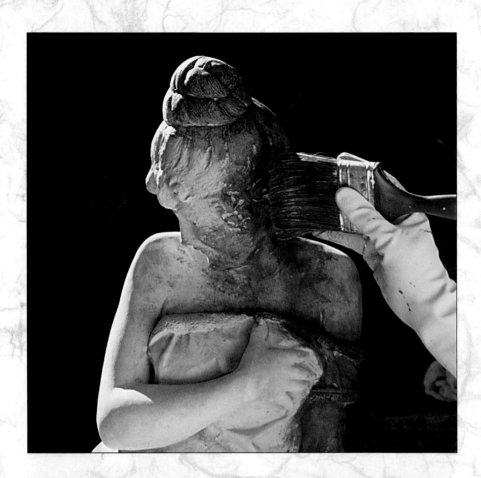

2 Using a 3-inch paintbrush (or a smaller brush if your concrete item is small), start painting at the top of the piece, working in small areas at a time. The paint absorbs very quickly into the cement, so be sure to quickly blend in any paint drips.

TIP: Do not overload your paintbrush. It is better to take your time and work slowly. Don't worry about getting the paint into any small creases at this point; they will be taken care of in Step 3.

3 In a separate small plastic container mix 1 part black paint with 1 part water. (A half cup of paint and a half cup of water is sufficient.)

Using a medium-sized artist's paintbrush, brush the black paint mixture into any recessed areas of the sculpture. This adds depth and gives the sculpture a more naturally aged look. (In our example, we added black paint to the folds of the dress, along the creases of the face, and so on.)

4 Let sculpture dry for 1 hour. Repeat Steps 2 and 3 until desired look is achieved. The patina of the sculpture will fade from the sun and rain, so it is better to start darker than lighter.

(If you live in an area with cold winters, it's a good idea either to move your statuary inside where it is dry, or to cover the item with plastic to keep moisture from seeping into your sculpture and then freezing when it gets cold. This can damage any concrete item.)

SPECIAL PROJECT TIP

Plain concrete garden ornaments can be found in many stores, including home improvement stores, hardware stores, and of course, lawn and garden stores. Consider applying this aging technique to garden urns, birdbaths, or even concrete garden animal statues such as rabbits or deer.

Welcome *Guests*

Want to make your guest room a bit more inviting? Let your linens greet visitors graciously.

Embroidered details on towels, linens, napkins, and sheets have long been a classic touch to show both pride of ownership and to add that little extra to home decor.

Today's newer sewing machines offer the elegance of embroidery at the touch of a switch. By selecting from a variety of preprogrammed stitches, you can permanently add these delightful details to your linens.

But if you don't have a newer sewing machine, there's another way to mimic this classic touch with only a few minutes' work.

In most craft and sewing stores, you can find premade, individual embroidered letters, each sold separately. These embroidery details come in several colors, and feature an iron-on backing that lets you attach them to fabric easily.

We decided to use these letters to add a simple touch to a set of guest linens by spelling out "Welcome Guests" on the edge of our pillowcases. Similar greetings such as "Our Friends," "Sleep Well," and a variety of other sentiments would be equally appropriate. (One added benefit of this is that it lets you spot the guest linens easily after doing wash. No more struggling to remember which set of sheets belongs to the guest room!)

This entire project only took about 20 minutes to finish. We selected white letters for a white background, and attached them to a set of vintage pillowcases.

You Will Need

- Iron-on embroidered letters to spell out a sentiment of your choice
- Sheets or pillowcases (cotton sheet sets are recommended)
- Iron and press cloth
- Needle
- Thread in a matching color

1 Remove the lettering from the packaging and place on your pillowcase or the edge of a sheet. Rearrange the letters until you have a shape that looks attractive to you. Carefully iron on one letter at a time, using a press cloth. Start from the beginning of the word, and make sure that the spacing between each letter is appropriate before continuing.

2 Although these iron-on letters can be washed, we wanted to make extra certain that the pieces would stay in place through multiple launderings. We used thread in a matching color to further secure the letters to our sheet using a simple overcast stitch.

Makeover *Magic*

With some basic tools and materials plus these clear, step-by-step instructions, you can transform a flea market cocktail table into an elegant ottoman, a few pieces of wood into functional furniture, or a dull-and-drab room into something truly special. Here's how to do it all yourself!

Flea Market *Treasure*

Transform an old side table into a button-tufted ottoman.

Button-tufted ottomans are a useful and attractive item in home decorating. They make wonderful stand-in cocktail tables, or provide extra seating when guests arrive. They also offer you a chance to bring complementary fabrics and textures into a room.

We found a simple way to make our own button-tufted ottoman for a few dollars out of a sturdy flea market table. (Make sure that the table you use for this project is structurally sound, with firm legs and strong wood, because people will tend to sit on this item of furniture; you want to make sure it will support the weight of a person.)

This project isn't difficult, but you may find it easier to enlist the support of a friend to help you stretch your fabric as you staple.

You Will Need

- Old cocktail table (ours was 18 inches wide, 32 inches long, and 16 inches tall)
- Measuring tape/yardstick
- Electric drill and ½-inch bit
- Marker
- 4-inch, high-density foam
- Upholstery batting to fit your table (this comes 28 inches wide, and is sold by the foot)
- 10-inch long upholstery needle

- Staple gun with ⅜-inch and ½-inch staples
- Spray adhesive
- 1 yard, 54-inch-wide fabric (or enough for your table)
- Scissors
- Flat fabric trim
- Fabric glue or hot-glue gun
- Prepackaged, covered button kit
- Strong cord
- Nail head trim
- Hammer/tacker

SPECIAL PROJECT TIP

Before you begin Step 1, draw a sketch of your table top to help you visualize where to put your tufted buttons. You want the buttons to be symmetrically placed on the surface of your ottoman. Below is a sketch of how we planned our button positioning.

SPECIAL PROJECT TIP

Before starting this project, be sure that the legs on the table you've selected are secure. If necessary, insert additional wood screws at each corner to improve stability. (The screws will be covered later with fabric.) Remove any loose veneer. If the table has a few scratches, sand the spots with fine steel wool and then apply a wood restorative product such as Old English or Restor A Finish, according to manufacturer's directions.

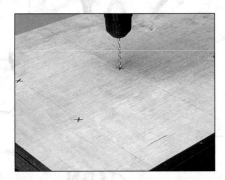

1 Measure the width and length of your table top. Our table was 18 inches wide and 32 inches long. You need to do a little math in order to make the button tufting symmetrical. Start by finding a number that divides equally into your table measurements. (See our sketch above for the button layout used on our table.)

Draw a grid on the top of the table and make an X at the button locations. Drill a hole about ½ inch in diameter at each mark. (NOTE: Our table had a shelf underneath which we removed until we had finished all of our upholstery.)

2 Measure and cut foam to the size of the table top. Spray adhesive on one side of the foam. Center foam on the table top. Press down foam to secure it in place.

3 Measure and cut upholstery batting 10 inches wider and 10 inches longer than your table top. Center the batting over the foam and staple in place using ⅜-inch staples. Start the staples at the center of one side. Repeat on the opposite side, pulling the batting taut while stapling. Repeat the same procedure on the ends. Go back and continue stapling, working from the center out toward the corners, leaving the corners unstapled. The staples should be about ½ inch apart. Ease the batting in at the corners and staple in place. Trim excess batting from edges and corners.

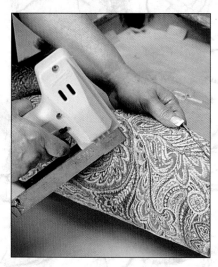

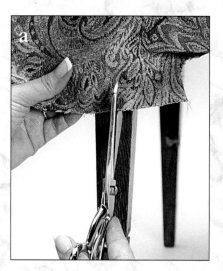

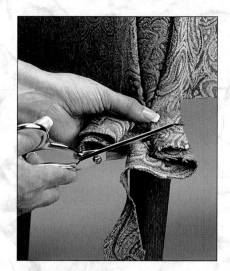

4 Measure the top of the table over the foam from bottom edge to bottom edge. Measure both the width and the length of the table and then add 6 inches to each measurement. Cut fabric to these dimensions. TIP: Be sure to check pattern placement, if any, before cutting the fabric.

Center the fabric on the table top and staple in place as in Step 3, stopping about 3 inches from each corner.

5 Pull fabric out and away from the corner, making excess fabric lie smooth and flat (photo 5a). Make a straight cut in the fabric starting about ½ inch out from the corner, stopping your cut even with the bottom rail of the table (photo 5b). Fold the raw edge under on the inside edge of the table leg. Pull fabric taut and staple in place, concealing the staples on the underside edge of the table top.

6 We decided to do a double miter at each corner to finish our fabric.

Start by smoothing the point of the fabric down at the corner, and then fold the excess fabric into a pleat on each side of the corner. Hold the fabric in place and trim excess fabric, allowing about 1 inch of excess length from the bottom edge of the table top.

SPECIAL PROJECT TIP

When purchasing fabric with a distinctive pattern, consider how that pattern will run on your ottoman. Some fabrics have a one-way pattern that may not work for your project.

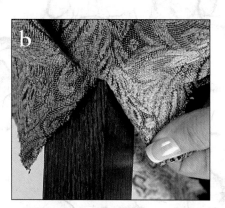

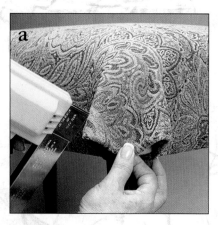

7 Once again, smooth down the point of the fabric at the corner and turn the raw edge under (photo 7a). Pull the fabric taut and staple in place on each side of the corner (photo 7b). NOTE: Keep the turned edge of the fabric even with the bottom edge of the table. Fold the excess fabric into a pleat on each side. Turn the raw edge of the fabric under and fold the pleats in toward the corner and staple in place (photo 7c). Keep staples within ½ inch of the bottom edge of the fabric. Repeat at remaining corners. NOTE: Depending on the thickness of your fabric, you may need to switch to ½-inch staples at the corners.

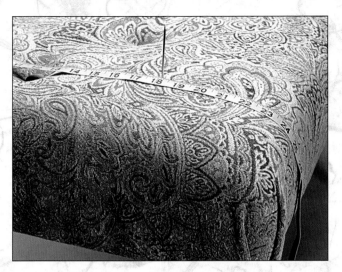

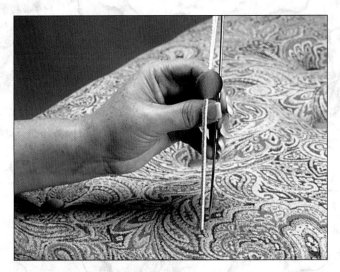

8 (Skip to Step 11 if you don't care to add tufted buttons to your ottoman.)

Prepare ready-to-cover fabric buttons following manufacturer's instructions. (Turn to page 111, Step 10, if you need help with this.) NOTE: Heavyweight fabrics don't work well with covered-button kits because the fabric is too thick to slide over the button. If you are using heavyweight fabric, as we did, use a contrasting or coordinating lightweight fabric to cover the buttons.

Double-thread a 10-inch upholstery needle with about 24 inches of strong cord. (Wrap the end of the cord with a piece of tape to thread through the eye of the needle.)

Insert the needle from the underside of the table up through the foam and fabric, double checking to ensure that the button placement is even with your original measurements.

9 Thread the button on the needle. Reinsert the needle next to the point of entry and push the needle back down through to the underside of the table top. SPECIAL PROJECT TIP: Bringing the needle back through the original hole in the table can sometimes be a challenge. If you're having trouble, try reinserting your needle at the point of entry on the top side. Then reach under the table and pull the cord taut. Continue pulling on the cord while you guide the needle back down through the point of entry. Pull the needle and cord completely through the hole, leaving a few inches of cord to work with on the bottom of your table. Cut the string to release the needle.

10 Lay the table on its side with the bottom of the table facing you. Holding all 4 strands of cord in one hand, reach around to the top side of your table and push on the button as you pull on the cord. Slowly pull the cords until you create the tuft on the top side. NOTE: The tension on the cord will let you know that you have pulled the cord to its maximum. Hold the tension on the cord in one hand while stapling the cord in place with the other. Fold the cord back and forth and continue to staple it in place. Trim excess cord and insert additional staples over the cord to keep it secure.

Repeat with remaining buttons, checking to ensure that all the buttons are symmetrical and that the tufting is even.

11 Use a fabric glue or a hot-glue gun to attach trim to the bottom edge of the fabric. This will cover the exposed staples on the ottoman. Starting at one corner of the ottoman, turn under the raw edge of the trim and glue in place. Continue around the entire ottoman, turning the raw edge under once again.

12 OPTIONAL: Nail head trim adds an inexpensive finishing touch to the ottoman. Start by tacking one nail head in at the corner. Insert additional tacks about 1/2 inch apart at the corners or around the entire ottoman.

SPECIAL PROJECT TIP

One specialty item that you'll need for this project is a 10-inch upholstery needle, which you can purchase at your local fabric store. A second handy item is a staple remover, which will help you remove damaged or misplaced staples as you work.

Stairs with *Flair*

Camouflage well-used wood stairs with an easy paint technique that mimics the appearance of landscape rock.

One of the challenges with this basement update was the wooden steps leading downstairs. Before the remodel, these stairs had been covered with old, stained carpet. The homeowners removed the carpeting but were left with the rough stairs.

One option would have been to recarpet, but the homeowners didn't like that idea. Resanding and refacing the steps was an expense they didn't want to take on at this point, although the wood itself was both gouged and pitted.

The solution? We decided to hide the disfigured wood with an easy faux-painting technique. In keeping with the "Paris apartment" feel the homeowners wanted, we created painted faux landscape rocks on the stairs, both brightening the stairway area, and giving the stairs a new lease on life.

You Will Need

- Primer (tinted gray—we used Zinsser 1-2-3, and had it tinted a rich charcoal gray at our local hardware store)
- Roll of 1-inch, easy-release painter's tape
- Utility knife
- Plastic gloves
- Light shade of acrylic enamel for the second base coat (we used a creamy yellow shade by Sherwin Williams)
- Acrylic craft paints in dark gray, chocolate brown, light gray, and gold
- Black marking pencil
- Oil-based polyurethane

SPECIAL PROJECT TIP

If you examine a piece of landscaping rock, you'll notice that the rock contains a variety of colors. Because we wanted our landscape rock to fit in with the colors in the basement, we selected shades that complemented the colors in the room.

Remember that the first coat of paint you apply will be the color of your grout—ours was a charcoal gray. The second coat will be the predominant color of your stones—ours were a creamy yellow. The accent colors you use to create definition and shade in your stones will be used sparingly, but will give the stones themselves character. We used acrylic craft paints in dark gray, chocolate brown, gold, and light gray.

You can experiment with the colors you select on an old board before proceeding to your stairs.

1 Be sure that the stairs are clean, dust-free, and dry. Tape walls around the edges of your stairs with painter's tape. Paint both the risers and the treads of your stairs with primer, tinted the color you wish the grout lines in your faux rocks to be. (We used charcoal gray as our first color.) Let dry completely, preferably overnight.

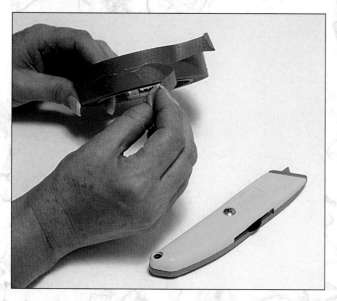

2 Select a roll of 1-inch, easy-release painter's tape. Working slowly and carefully, use a utility knife to score lightly through the center of the tape, leaving a smooth, rolling edge. (This will give you two pieces of tape, each about ½ inch wide. The uneven edges of the tape will make your grout lines appear more natural.)

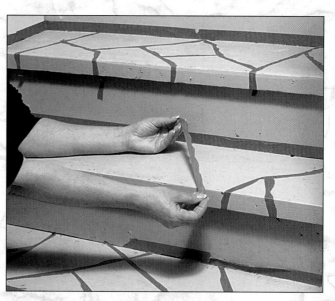

3 Begin placing your tape across the tread of each stair, making a random pattern over the painted surface. Create angles and edges, making some "stones" larger and others smaller. A random pattern looks most natural. As you work, look at the pattern on the previous stair, making sure that you vary the placement of the tape from area to area. Make sure you extend your tape over the front edge of the step lip, stopping above the riser on the stair below you.

4 Once you've taped all of your stairs, it's time to apply the second, contrasting coat of paint. We used a creamy yellow. Brush your paint directly over the painter's tape lines, applying a thorough but thin coat.
   Let dry.

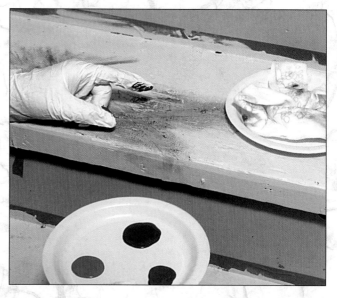

5 Place a dab of chocolate brown, dark gray, gold, and light gray acrylic paint on a plastic plate. On a separate plate nearby, put about half a dozen damp paper towels.
   Put on plastic gloves, and use your finger to pick up a little of the dark gray paint. A tiny bit of paint is all you need. Using your finger, start at the outside edge of a rock (next to the painter's tape grout line) and swirl the paint over the yellow base coat. Move quickly, spreading the paint with your gloved fingers. You want to create a darker shadow near the edge of your stones. If you accidentally apply too much paint, or want a lighter area, use a damp paper towel to wipe off the excess.
   Continue this process for several steps, always moving quickly and varying the intensity of the shade from stone to stone.

6 Continue this process with the other colors on your tray. You don't want any one stone to be shaded exactly like another. Vary the intensity and shades of the stones as you move.

To give your stairs a warmer patina, you can dip a fairly wet paper towel into a bit of the chocolate brown paint and "wash" the color across all of the stones.

7 Once you are pleased with the appearance of your stones, remove the painter's tape. Peel the tape up gently, taking care not to disturb the base coat of primer underneath.

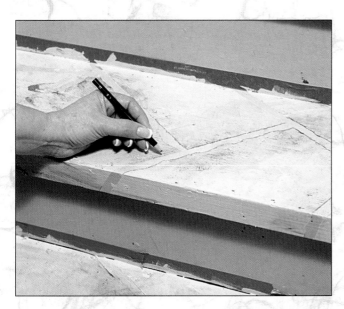

8 Use a colored marking pencil to lightly sketch around the edges of your grout lines. You don't need to be exact; a simple but light outline is enough to make the grout lines more prominent. Examine each stone as you outline. This is a chance to add a bit more paint to any area that needs to be further defined.

As a final step, to protect the faux painting on your steps, seal the paint with several light coats of polyurethane, following manufacturer's instructions.

Sitting *Pretty*

These adorable skirted kids' ottomans, designed for use around a small play table, will let your favorite little person sit in style.

Creative play is soothing for people of any age. This fun project will let you create cute child-size ottomans for a bedroom or play area. You can use any fabrics you wish to match a bedspread, curtains, or any other decorative detail in a room.

(It's a good idea to protect the fabric on these finished ottomans with a fabric protector, especially in children's rooms.)

SPECIAL PROJECT TIP

Prefabricated tapered legs generally come in 6-, 8-, and 12-inch lengths. For our table, we cut 1 inch off the bottom of each 12-inch leg to accommodate our desired ottoman height.

You Will Need

The materials here will make four ottomans that are 15 inches tall, 14 inches wide, and 12 inches deep. They fit around a child's table that is 22 inches tall, 40 inches wide, and 24 inches deep.

For the base:
- One 10-foot long, 12-inch wide piece of pine lumber (this should be cut into eight pieces, each 14 inches long, with a piece of scrap left over)*

For the seat tops:
- 2-inch high density foam for seat tops
- Foam spray adhesive
- 2½ yards of upholstery batting (this is generally 27 inches wide; do not use quilt batting for this project)
- Staple gun
- 1¼ yards of decorative fabric for seat tops
- Sixteen 12-inch tapered legs with straight top plates (available at your local home improvement center)

- Drill and 1¼-inch wood screws
- 3 yards of fabric for the ottoman skirts (we purchased 1½ yards of two different fabrics)
- 3 yards of lining fabric
- 6 yards of trim cord with a lip (we purchased two different colors)
- 6 yards of flat trim or gimp
- Cardboard tacking strip (available at your local fabric outlet)

Miscellaneous supplies:
- Glue gun and glue
- Pins and measuring tape
- Scissors

You can have the lumber precut at your local home improvement store for a small charge if you wish.

2 Select four additional pieces of your precut lumber. (Do not use the seat tops from Step 1.) To attach legs to the ottoman base, position the top plates from your purchased legs ¾ inch in from outside edges on all four corners. Mark the screw locations with a marker. Create a starting mark for the screws using an awl and attach top plates to the ottoman base (photo 2a). Screw legs in place (photo 2b). (This base will be attached to your padded seat tops in a later step.)

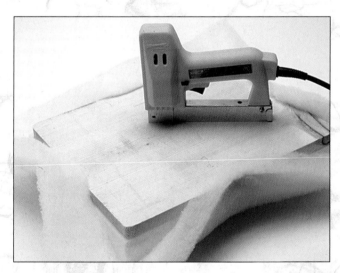

1 (NOTE: These directions make four ottomans; to make fewer, adjust your materials accordingly.)

Cut four pieces of foam equal to the size of your ottoman seats. Spray a seat with foam adhesive. Place foam on seat, lining up edges. Repeat for additional seats.

Cut four pieces of upholstery batting 4 inches wider and longer than the seat tops. Place batting on your work surface and center each seat on the batting, foam side down. Staple the batting in place, securing it at the center on all sides.

Working from the center out, continue stapling batting in place, keeping staples about ½ inch apart, stopping 2 inches from each corner. NOTE: Pull the batting taut as you work from side to side.

Gather and fold the excess material at the corners and staple in place. Trim excess batting. Repeat the same process over the top of your batting with decorative fabric. Set the tops aside for the moment.

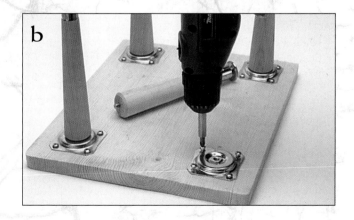

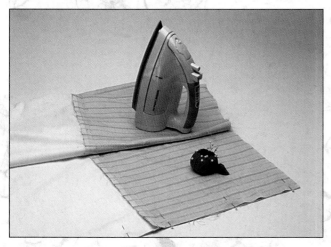

3 To make a skirt for the ottoman base from Step 2, measure the height of the ottoman from the floor to the top of the wooden seat and add 2½ inches for seam allowances, hems, and tacking to the top of the seat.

For the fabric width, double the perimeter of the seat to allow for box pleating at the corners. Cut four pieces of decorative fabric equal to these measurements.

Cut four pieces of lining fabric 1 inch shorter in length and equal in width to the above measurements. (The fabric for our skirt was railroaded, which means the design runs horizontally from edge to edge. If this is not true of the fabric you select, simply sew widths together to meet your measurements before you attach the lining.) NOTE: You don't have to line the skirt of the ottoman, but using lining gives the skirt more body and also eliminates seeing any stitching.

Pin lining to your decorative fabric, lining up the raw edges along the long side, with right sides together. Sew using a ½-inch seam allowance and press. With right sides together, seam the two short sides together, and press.

Fold fabric in half along the length, lining up raw edges and press; this turns under the decorative fabric creating a hem.

4 Fit the skirt to the ottoman base by pinning the fabric around the seat of the ottoman, box pleating 12 inches (6 inches per side) of fabric at each corner. Work your way around the ottoman, making any small adjustments needed so that the skirt fits tightly around the seat.

5 Bring the raw edge of the skirt to the top of the seat and staple in place, leaving a ½-inch space between the bottom of the skirt and your work surface. This will allow room for the skirt to hang freely above a carpeted floor. If the ottomans will be used on a hard surface, such as hardwood flooring, vinyl, or tile, reduce this space to ¼ inch.

When stapling, start in the center and work your way out to the corners on each side of the seat.

6 Attach the ottoman top to the base by placing the top of the ottoman, upholstered side down, on your surface. Center the base over the top and attach using 1¼-inch wood screws.

7 Cut a strip of fabric 3 inches wide and the perimeter of the ottoman plus 4 inches long. (Ours was 3 inches by 54 inches.)

Press a ¾-inch hem along the long side of the strip toward the wrong side of the fabric. Sew the cording to the right side of the fabric along the length of the strip, lining up the edge of the cording with the raw edge of the fabric.

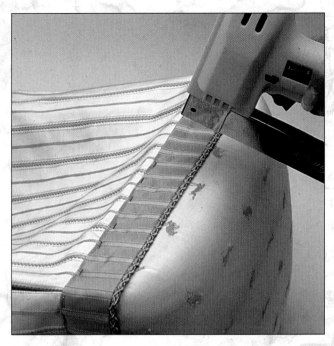

8 Staple the strip of fabric in place, wrong side down, starting in the center of one side of the ottoman. The cording should sit even with the top rim of the seat. Insert a few staples about 1 inch apart, working in a 6-inch section at a time (photo 8a). (TIP: Measure from the corded edge to the bottom rim of the seat to ensure that the cording is kept straight.)

Place the cardboard tacking strip snugly against the edge of the cording and staple in place (photo 8b). Continue around the perimeter of the ottoman. Neatly turn the end of the raw edge of the fabric and cording under and staple in place.

9 Flip the strip of fabric over, exposing the right side, and staple in place. The edge of the fabric should sit just above the rim of the bottom of the seat.

SPECIAL PROJECT TIP

Once you have established the placement of the skirt on the top of the ottoman, measure from the edge of the seat to the raw edge of the fabric. Remove the skirt and draw a line around the perimeter of the seat equal to this measurement. Use this line as a guide for the skirt placement.

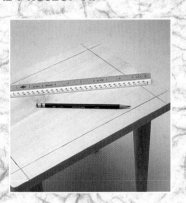

10 Hot-glue trim in place, covering the exposed staples. The edge of the trim should sit even with the rim of the bottom of the seat.

A Room with a *View*

To turn a cramped stairway into a welcoming entryway for a basement room, consider adding visual details that surprise and delight.

We added two distinctive details to this room—a water-transfer mural, and a rub-on quote in French on the sloped ceiling.

If you've ever watched someone make a model airplane, you'll be familiar with the idea behind the wet-transfer mural of a window scene we used. (These murals are much like the small model decals that you apply after wetting the backing.)

The two-piece mural we selected (the window and the decorative stone archway surrounding it), is recommended for use on flat, painted surfaces. However, you can apply these murals to other surfaces for a different end result.

We applied our mural to a painted wall with a slightly rough "orange peel" surface. The result is that as the mural dried, small horizontal cracks appeared throughout the image. We liked the aged effect this produced on our mural, which made it seem as if it had been handpainted with oil paints long ago.

The mural comes complete with a color, full-size image of the finished piece. We cut this out and positioned it on our wall until we were happy with the placement. We then followed manufacturer's directions to apply the actual window scene to our wall area. Once the piece is secured in place, the back of the mural is dampened repeatedly with a wet sponge, gently releasing the image portion of the mural from its backing paper. Once the mural has separated from the paper, the backing piece is carefully peeled off to leave the image attached on the wall. We found it helpful to gently pat the mural against the wall with a damp cloth, ensuring that it attached well to our slightly rough orange peel surface. We then applied the decorative stone arch around our image the same way.

Wall Mural

We ordered our wall mural from a company called Tarantelli Designs (www.tarantellidesigns.com). Our large, two-piece mural cost about $135, including shipping.

You Will Need

- Wet-application wall mural
- Easy-release blue painter's tape
- Measuring tape
- Pencil
- Bucket
- Sponge

Clever Quote

We ordered our quote, a French sentence that means "Eat well, laugh often, and love long" from a company called Wall Words (www.wallwords.com) for about $35. This company makes premade, plastic-backed, rub-on lettering and phrases in a variety of styles and colors. You can contact them at (888)422-6685.

You Will Need

- Press-on lettering
- Easy-release blue painter's tape
- A measuring tape
- Pencil
- Chunky stamp (we used a fleur-de-lis stamp made by Duncan)
- Gold craft paint
- Brown craft paint

1 Be sure that the wall where you wish to attach your quote is clean and dry. If you have recently painted the surface, wait a day or two before attaching your quote to that area.

Decide where you wish to apply your quote. You'll need to measure the length of your actual phrase, measure the surface where you want to apply it, and then plan how the quote will look in that area.

With our quote, we decided to apply it in four lines. That meant cutting one line into two pieces between words.

To visualize how our quote would appear, we took four pieces of painter's tape, cut to the rough size of each line of our quote, and positioned them on our sloped ceiling. (Measure the distances between lines and carefully center the lines between the side walls.)

2 Once you're satisfied with your positioning, you need to prepare the lettering. On the Wall Words' product we used, the quote had a backing sheet of slippery paper, the rub-on letters, and then a clear sheet of plastic to which the letters were attached. Manufacturer's instructions call for burnishing the letters (rubbing them with a blunt, hard tool such as a paint stir stick) to make sure that the letters are firmly attached to the clear backing.

Once you've done this, tape your quote to the wall and remove the protective white paper back.

3 Transfer the lettering to the wall by rubbing vigorously on the plastic backing with your burnishing stick. We also found it helpful to rub the entire surface a second time with a cloth to ensure that our letters adhered firmly. Once you've transferred the lettering, remove the plastic back.

4 We added detail to our quote by stamping fleur-de-lis images between each line. We used a paintbrush to apply a thin layer of gold craft paint to our stamp, and then added a bit of chocolate brown paint around the edges of the stamp to add variation. Press firmly to the wall, without sliding the stamp from side to side, and then remove. If you make a mistake, you can wash the paint off the wall immediately with a wet cloth and try again.

A Blanket *Chest*

This inexpensive, sturdy storage chest is made from one sheet of plywood, and fabric. The cost? Less than $100 and just a few hours' work.

The pleasure of color-coordinating a piece of uphol-stered furniture to match the fabric in a room is a treat that usually requires a lot of cash.

That's not the case with this project.

You can make this blanket chest with minimal skills for a very reasonable price. Best of all, you can select the fabric to cover your chest, matching the finished item to your curtains, your bedding, or any other piece of decor.

This sturdy chest can also double as a seat, which makes it particularly nice at the foot of the bed as a place to sit while you dress.

You Will Need

- One ¾-inch thick, 4-by-8-foot sheet of A/B plywood (See Special Project Note below.)
- Sandpaper
- 2¼ yards of blackout lining fabric
- Two sheets of ½-inch foam
- Scissors
- Fabric spray adhesive
- Drill with ⅛- and ⁵⁄₃₂-inch drill bits
- Wood glue and wood filler
- No. 8 1½-inch wood screws/wallboard screws

- Foam adhesive
- 3 yards of medium-weight decorative fabric to wrap the chest (See Special Project Note below.)
- Electric staple gun with ⅜-inch staples
- 8 yards of gimp/trim
- Hot-glue gun and glue
- One 24-by-48-inch piece of 2-inch foam for the lid
- 54-inch long upholstery-weight Dacron

- 1¼ yards medium-weight coordinating decorative fabric for lid
- 3 brass hinges and screws
- 2 friction lid supports—right-hand and left-hand mount
- Phillips screwdriver

Optional:
- 4 brass casters with mounting plates
- No. 8 ¾-inch screws

SPECIAL PROJECT NOTE

At our local home improvement store, our plywood cost less than $30. (A/B means that the wood is smooth on one side, with no knotholes or other imperfections. This makes putting fabric on it much easier.) While we were at the store, we had the wood cut into the pieces we needed for a minimal price, less than $5. (Smaller pieces of wood are also easier to transport.)

For this project, it works best to purchase a fabric that can be railroaded to wrap the chest; otherwise you will need to cut the fabric and create seams at the front corners of the chest. Railroading simply means that the fabric can run along its width without altering the pattern.

Cutting instructions for the plywood:
- Cut one front and one back—16 by 47 inches
- Cut one bottom—19 by 45½ inches
- Cut two sides—16 by 19 inches
- Cut one lid—21 by 48 inches

IMPORTANT Note:
Be sure to check the thickness of your plywood before cutting the bottom of chest in order to ensure that the bottom dimensions are accurate.

The measurement of the bottom from side to side should be equal to 47 inches minus twice the thickness of the plywood.

1 Sand all cut edges and surfaces of your wood pieces smooth.

We applied a fabric called blackout lining to all the inside faces of the wood for our chest except the lid to create a smooth, clean surface. We also added ½-inch foam to the outside faces of our cut wood to give the finished chest a softer shape.

To do this, place all cut plywood pieces except the lid on the wrong side of blackout lining and trace outlines with a pencil.

Repeat tracing on ½-inch foam.

Cut out all lining and foam pieces and set foam aside. Spray fabric adhesive on wrong side of lining; affix lining to the smooth side of the plywood on all pieces (these will be inside your box).

	For example:
	47 inches
minus	¾ inch
minus	¾ inch
equals	45½ inches

Order of assembly
1. Sides to bottom
2. Front to sides and bottom
3. Back to sides and bottom

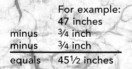

SIDE   SIDE   FRONT   BACK

BOTTOM

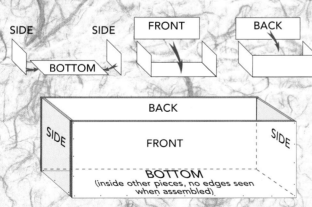

BACK

SIDE   FRONT   SIDE

BOTTOM
(inside other pieces, no edges seen when assembled)

Finished measurement of the unupholstered chest is 47 inches wide, 19 inches deep, and 16 inches high.

2 NOTE: These next few steps are easier if you have a helper.

Attach one side piece to the bottom of the chest, aligning lower edges and sides to the bottom piece. Pre-drill three holes starting about 1 inch from the top and bottom, as well as the middle, using a $^5/_{32}$-inch drill bit.

Apply a line of wood glue at the joint. Align edges and secure with wood screws. Repeat on opposite side. TIP: Be careful not to drill holes too deep or the screws will not grab. To avoid this, place a piece of tape on the drill bit about 1 inch from the tip, and stop drilling when you reach this mark.

3 Stand chest on end. Position the front on the box, aligning side and bottom edges. Drill holes as described in Step 2, adding additional screws in the middle. Apply a line of wood glue at the joints. Align edges and secure with wood screws. Repeat for back piece.

Attach cut pieces of $^1/_2$-inch foam to the outside of the box using the foam adhesive. Follow manufacturer's instructions when using the foam adhesive.

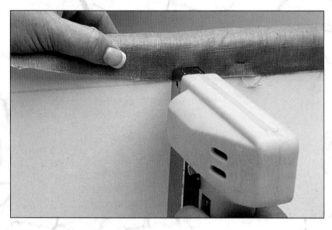
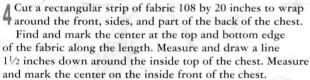

4 Cut a rectangular strip of fabric 108 by 20 inches to wrap around the front, sides, and part of the back of the chest.

Find and mark the center at the top and bottom edge of the fabric along the length. Measure and draw a line 1½ inches down around the inside top of the chest. Measure and mark the center on the inside front of the chest.

Line up the center markings of the fabric and the chest. Align the raw edge of the fabric with the line on the inside of the chest and staple in place. Continue to staple fabric around the top edge, inserting staples about every 3 inches. Once all fabric is stapled in place, go back and insert additional staples, keeping staples about ¼ inch apart. Turn chest over and staple fabric in place on underside of chest, gently pulling the fabric as you staple.

5 To finish the back of the chest, cut a strip of fabric 45 by 20 inches. Press under a 1-inch hem along the sides to conceal the raw edges.

Measure and mark the center of the fabric as well as the inside back and bottom of the box (photo 5a). Staple the fabric in place, following the same instructions from Step 4. Hot-glue the gimp/trim in place over the staples and raw edge of the fabric on the inside of the chest (photo 5b).

6 Cut a piece of blackout lining fabric 1 inch smaller in width and length than the outside bottom of the chest. Apply fabric spray adhesive to the lining fabric. Center and affix the fabric to the bottom of the chest. Staple the fabric in place along the outside edges to ensure that it is securely in place.

SPECIAL PROJECT TIP

As you reach the corners of your chest, insert a staple to hold fabric in place. Miter fold fabric over the exposed staple and insert staple on inside of the chest.

7 To cover the lid, place the 2-inch foam on your work surface. Place the lid on foam and trim to size. Spray lid with foam adhesive and affix foam, lining up the edge of the foam with the edges of the lid.

Lay upholstery-weight Dacron on work surface and center lid on the Dacron, foam-side down. Staple the Dacron in place, working from the center out on one side, stopping about 2 inches from each side at the corner, keeping staples approximately 1/2 inch apart. Repeat on opposite side, pulling the Dacron taut as you staple it in place.

Repeat this process for each side. Gather and fold the excess Dacron at the corners and staple in place, ensuring that the hard edge of the corner has been softened by the Dacron. Trim excess. Repeat the same process with the decorative fabric. Trim excess.

To finish the inside of the lid, cut a piece of the fabric used to wrap the chest 1 inch smaller than the width and length of the lid. Staple the fabric in place, following the same process; working from side to side, pulling the fabric taut as you go. Keep staples 1/2 inch apart.

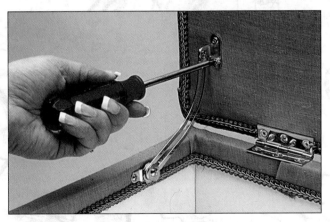

8 Mark locations for hinges at the back of the chest starting about 5 inches in from each side, as well as one hinge in the middle. Pre-drill using 1/8-inch drill bit; install hinges.

Hot-glue gimp/trim in place over the staples and raw edge of the fabric. TIP: It is very easy to strip brass screws when using a drill. You may want to use a Phillips screwdriver to attach your hinges.

9 Center the back edge of the lid with the back edge of the chest. Mark screw locations for the hinges; pre-drill holes using 1/8-inch drill bit. Reposition the lid and secure hinges. Install lid supports according to manufacturer's instructions. (These prevent the lid from accidentally slamming shut, and provide friction so that the lid must be gently pressed closed.)

If you like, you can attach casters to the bottom of your chest to make it easy to move. (You'll need casters that mount flat against a surface with a metal plate.)

Quick Kitchen *Makeover*

Update a kitchen for minimal expense using these do-it-yourself tricks for saving cash.

When it comes to do-it-yourself dilemmas, few rooms are as difficult as a kitchen. Often the center of the house and the heart of our entertaining area, kitchen remodels can be tremendously expensive and a lot of work. Older kitchens also generally suffer from the same problems—a dated look, too little storage, a lack of counter space, and so on.

Those challenges certainly existed in this kitchen, a 1950s rambler that had good bones but a tired face.

We decided to see how some creativity, a little cash, and a

Before

few weekends of hard work could transform this space into a cozy, updated kitchen. We planned to do the majority of the work ourselves, using simple carpentry skills, painting, and tile cutting and installation. (NOTE: If you hire out any of the work involved with your project, your costs will rise, but it might be worth it to you for peace of mind. That choice is yours.)

Start with the basics
In order for any room update or remodeling to be successful, you need a plan.

1 Start with your wish list. Write down everything you're dreaming about. More cupboards? Write it down. A new floor? Add that too. This isn't the time to think about budgets— this is the time for thinking big.

2 Now it's time to set priorities. For each item on your list, assign a number that corresponds with how important it is to you to have that problem fixed right now. You'll find that costs escalate quickly with a project like this, so make sure you spend your budget—whatever the amount —on the items from which you'll get the most satisfaction.

Spend money wisely
Granite and other solid-surface countertops are gorgeous, but they are also expensive. Because this project was under tight budget constraints, we chose a laminate countertop in a neutral shade, but then splurged a bit with a few expensive decorative tiles inset in our backsplash.

3 Determine how much cash you're actually able to spend on your project. For this kitchen, we had a budget of $5,000, and our priority list looked like this: 1) New appliances; 2) New countertop; 3) New lights; 4) Updated cabinets; 5) Additional storage; 6) New paint and cosmetic updates; 7) New floor.

With any do-it-yourself project, you need to be honest with yourself about your skills and your ability to trade time for money. We knew we would need to hire an electrician to replace lights, so we budgeted for that expense. If you've never installed tile before, you might consider hiring an experienced installer to handle that portion of your project. If you hate to paint, budget for that expense. Also, if you need your project finished by a certain date, remember that saving money also generally means the project moves at a slower pace. Keep that in mind.

Trim work/or moldings

Many of the updates in this kitchen came from adding simple details to our existing cabinetry and woodwork. Premade trim comes in many shapes and sizes that can complement any decor and is readily available at most home improvement stores.

For our cabinets, we used premade molding in layers on all our existing doors and drawers. We used a miter box to cut the moldings to size, and then glued and nailed them in place.

We also added a thin strip of molding below our cabinet fronts to hide the undercabinet light fixtures.

Creative designs can be achieved by

Makeover Budget—$5,000

Before

THE BUDGET—$5,000

Appliances—$1,895 (We shopped at a discount warehouse and found a package deal for the fridge, stove, and dishwasher)

LAMINATE COUNTERTOP—$400 (We purchased this, cut to size, from a home improvement store)

LIGHTING—$150 (We selected simple but utilitarian fixtures)

TRIM WORK & MOLDING —$425 (We purchased a variety of inexpensive moldings from a home improvement store and then layered them on our cabinets for an updated appearance and added crown molding around our ceiling)

ONE NEW CABINET—$35 (We did some scrounging at an architectural salvage yard and found an unfinished cabinet that matched the style of the existing units)

MISC. LUMBER—$125 (We finished the sides of our new cabinet and made new book shelves for one wall)

DRYWALL & SUPPLIES—$75

TWO DECORATIVE CORBELS—$40 (We purchased resin corbels rather than wood from a company called Outwater Plastics and then painted them ourselves)

PAINT & SUPPLIES—$125 (We layered our paint with a faux painting technique to bring some warmth to the room)

BACKSPLASH—$150 (We purchased inexpensive field tile for the majority of the backsplash and then splurged on a few expensive accent tile pieces)

FLOOR TILE—$700 (We shopped discount tile shops/salvage yards to find our floor tile. With some judicious shopping, you can find excellent tiles for as little as $2.50/square foot.)

TILE CUTTER RENTAL—$55 (We rented this from our local home improvement store. You'll often also find classes available at these stores to show you how to use the equipment.)

SINK & FAUCET—$80 (We found these at our local home improvement store)

NEW CABINET HARDWARE—$60 (We shopped the discount table at our local cabinet shop)

DRAPERY & RODS—$150 (We bought ready-made drapery)

ELECTRICIAN—$320 (Always hire licensed technicians)

TOTAL SPENT—$4,985

Make use of extra space

Inexpensive open bookshelves— we added the simple ones shown here—are a great way to make use of space that might otherwise be wasted on a wall. These are also a great way to create more storage options, particularly important in a small kitchen.

Consider crowns

Adding crown molding to a ceiling is a finishing touch that doesn't need to be expensive. Instead of paying for wood crown molding, investigate resin moldings, which are less expensive and lightweight.

Small details make a difference

Adding undercabinet lights makes any kitchen feel more welcoming. To disguise the undercabinet fixtures, we added a simple wood rail to the bottom of the cabinet.

Use decor that dazzles

Use items from other areas in your house in unusual ways in the kitchen to create an impact. Here a small table tucked into a corner offers a chance to add a table lamp and other decorative details that make the kitchen seem cozy and warm.

Inexpensive wood trim gives old cabinets a facelift

New cabinets can be one of the most expensive portions of a kitchen update. Instead of replacing dated cabinetry, try removing the doors and drawer fronts, and then add inexpensive wood trim from your local home improvement store to give them an instant update. Cut the trim to size (photo a), glue it in place (photo b), and then secure with small nails (photo c). Sand them, paint or stain to match, and you're done.

layering two or three different types of moldings. Take a little time to browse in the millwork department at your local home improvement store. Buy a few different pieces and bring them home to experiment with; many are priced by the linear foot and others are priced by the 8-foot piece.

For our crown molding around the ceiling, we saved considerable money by purchasing and installing resin moldings. These products, available at your local home improvement store, are prefabricated plastic-like products that have the look of wood, but are less expensive.

Reuse and recycle
To add storage to a kitchen, consider shopping around at local salvage shops for an old kitchen cabinet frame. If you have the space, this can be mounted in the kitchen, and then updated with trim and paint to match your existing cabinetry. For a finishing touch on all the cabinetry, install new drawer and handle pulls.

Adding additional storage
This kitchen lacked storage space, so we added more room by placing a salvaged kitchen cabinet above our stove. (Be sure to check any local regulations regarding placement of such cabinets.)

Because this cabinet was a salvaged piece, we added additional trim and beadboard to the sides to give the piece a finished look. We also placed resin corbels under either side of the cabinet to give it a finishing, decorative touch.

Finally, we painted the kitchen walls with a faux technique that blended several warm colors, including hints of red. We added a bookcase

to one corner of the room, along with an armchair to provide a place to relax and read, and then finished our room with a few decorative accents to complete our update.

SPECIAL PROJECT TIP

With any remodeling project, always leave room for unforeseen challenges—about 10 to 20 percent of the budget, just in case.

SPECIAL PROJECT TIP

Before starting any home improvement project, always check with your local city office to determine whether permits are required for any of your planned projects. If permits are required, be sure to include the cost of the permits in your budget.

Before

Index